YOU'RE DEAD—SO WHAT?

YOU'RE DEAD— SO WHAT?

Media, Police, and the Invisibility of Black Women as Victims of Homicide

Cheryl L. Neely

Michigan State University Press
East Lansing

♾ The paper used in this publication meets the minimum requirements of ANSI/NISO
Z39.48-1992 (R 1997) (Permanence of Paper).

Michigan State University Press
East Lansing, Michigan 48823-5245

Printed and bound in the United States of America.

21 20 19 18 17 16 15 1 2 3 4 5 6 7 8 9 10

Library of Congress Control Number: 2015933885
ISBN: 978-1-61186-178-5 (pbk.)
ISBN: 978-1-60917-465-1 (ebook: PDF)
ISBN: 978-1-62895-237-7 (ebook: ePub)
ISBN: 978-1-62896-237-6 (ebook: Kindle)

Book design by Scribe Inc. (www.scribenet.com)
Cover design by Shaun Allshouse (www.shaunallshouse.com)

green press INITIATIVE Michigan State University Press is a member of the Green Press Initiative and
is committed to developing and encouraging ecologically responsible publishing
practices. For more information about the Green Press Initiative and the use of recycled
paper in book publishing, please visit www.greenpressinitiative.org.

Visit Michigan State University Press at www.msupress.org

To Michelle . . . for a life now gone,
for children never born, for a smile that has faded to
memory . . . you remain in the hearts of all of us who loved you.

CONTENTS

ACKNOWLEDGMENTS

WHEN CONDUCTING RESEARCH ON SUCH AN EMOTIONALLY DIFFICULT topic as the tragic murders of women, there were times when I leaned on my God and Savior to steady me when reading accounts of homicides that literally left me speechless. I am grateful for my faith.

I want to thank a number of people who helped make this book possible. First of all, I would like to thank my daughter, Jewell, for her continued support and urging in writing this manuscript, and her provocative reminder that I did not just complete a Ph.D. to have the title of doctor. "You also need to make an impact with your research and write that book!" she told me on several occasions. Moreover, it was my daughter who came up with the title of this book, "Your Dead—So What?" I would also like to thank my husband, Carlespie, who not only assisted me with my analysis on the dissertation that shaped this book but also read and re-read my manuscript and offered thoughtful critique and encouragement throughout the process of writing. I would also like to thank my many students who routinely ask when the book will be published and continue to express a genuine interest in reading it. In particular, I want to thank Rochelle Chapman, the student who connected me again with Michelle Jackson's family. I am inclined to believe it was destiny that brought you to my class that day.

I want to thank Officers Frank Gregory and Brandon Lewis, of the

Acknowledgments

Detroit police department; Detective Lieutenant Robert Grant, from the Brownstown Township police department; and Sergeant Kenneth Gardner, of the homicide division of the Detroit police department, for graciously agreeing to be interviewed for the book and consistently working hard to bring justice to victims of violent crime. I also want to thank Gina McCauley and her blog "What About Our Daughters" for using alternative forms of media to engage in social activism on behalf of invisible women of color who are murdered and/or missing.

I am forever indebted to the family of Michelle Jackson, specifically her mother, Carlotta, and her cousin, Jodie Kenney, who opened up their hearts and embraced my project, despite the pain it caused them to relive Michelle's brutal death.

I am committed to bringing justice for my beautiful friend and some semblance of closure to her aggrieved family after thirty years with no resolution. I thank them for providing photos of Michelle for the manuscript . . . seeing her smile after all this time was an emotionally powerful moment for me. It was my goal to provide pictures of all of the victims mentioned in my book, but the logistics of contacting victims' families who were emotionally traumatized by the murders of their loved ones required more fortitude than I could muster. I strongly encourage readers to Google the images of the victims to provide a visual of these young women whose lives ended too soon.

I would like to thank my sisters, Cassandra Bell and Kimberly Neely, for their encouragement and excitement about this project. Cassandra, it moved me when you said, "You never forgot Michelle after all these years." I did not. I would also like to thank Elise Jajuga of the Michigan State University Press for her infallible assistance in editing the final manuscript. Her keen scrutiny is most appreciated. And finally, I want to thank my editor, J. Alex Schwartz, for championing this book and providing insight and feedback that motivated me every step of the way. Our coffeehouse conversations will never be forgotten.

INTRODUCTION

To make the case that the media and law enforcement offi-
cers often ignore black women as victims of homicide, I believe it is important
first to make clear to the reader what I mean by the term "invisibility." Obvi-
ously, the term is not to be taken in the literal sense, but to connote society's
attempt to render black women as inconspicuous and obscure, to marginal-
ize the importance of their life experiences in a white society.

In a patriarchal (male-dominated) society, the lives of women have less
value than those of men. The devaluing of women's lives is even further compounded when one factors in race and social class. Black women not only
face sexism as females, but they also are discriminated against on the basis of
race and class. A number of black feminist scholars and writers have documented the historical pattern of white society rendering black women as
invisible, particularly as it relates to their powerlessness as both women and
minorities.[1] To suggest that all women are discriminated against equally
is naive, to say the least, and virtually ignores the impact that race has in
facilitating black women's marginalization. As I have stated to my students
many times in my lectures on racial discrimination, when people look at me,
they see a "black woman"—not "woman black." Race remains a powerful
organizer of social life in the United States, but studies on race primarily
concentrate on the experiences of black men.

The novelist and activist Alice Walker is one of several black feminists who promoted a separation of black feminism from the mainstream white feminist agenda, which they believed fell short in adequately addressing pivotal issues in black women's lives.[2] For example, African American women have experienced more disenfranchisement as females in a male-dominated society than their white counterparts because of race. This disparity impacts their life chances, their opportunities for social mobility, and, even more troubling, their crime victimization rate.[3] Black women have lives that are "unique and significantly divergent" from those of white women, but most feminist perspectives do not consider that issues of race create a whole other level of complexity in black women's struggles for autonomy.[4] Doors that open to white women close in the faces of African American women because of racial discrimination. Therefore a simple call for equal rights for women is, in short, useless for black women unless those rights also address racism.

The result of this obscurity has been a "third wave" of the feminist movement by African American feminists—one that seeks to amplify the movement's need to address the multiple levels of inequality black women encounter along the lines of sex, race, and class. Thus, black women step up to the plate to bat with three strikes against them. As such, they never really get to participate in society as full-fledged team members.[5] Moreover, the movement attempts to address black women's struggles in carving out an identity without the stereotypes that have dogged them for centuries. In sum, these movements work actively to make the invisible visible.

The sociologist Patricia Hill Collins has sought to explain the unique position of African American women and argues that all women's experiences with sexism are not universal—black women also face discrimination based on three intersecting levels of oppression—race, sex, and social class.[6] In her article "The Tie That Binds: Race, Gender, and U.S. violence," Hill-Collins examines how the intersecting domains of racism, sexism, and classism contribute to black women's encounters with violence as gender and racial hierarchies are legitimated through the portrayal of certain types of violence in the media.[7] For example, the stereotype of black women as emasculating and confrontational in relationships justifies domestic violence as their abusers are seen as men pushed to the point of losing control.

Additionally, Hill-Collins argues that black women's issues with violence are ignored when racial violence focuses on black men and gender violence focuses on white women. For instance, accounts of racial profiling and race-related assaults and/or homicides tend to highlight black men as victims, while stories of domestic/lethal intimate violence feature white women as primary victims. Therefore, race- or gender-only approaches eclipse black women's experiences as victims of violence and are limited in explaining their unique position of vulnerability. Furthermore, these feelings of vulnerability are rooted in a historical context—namely, the inherent bias in the criminal justice system since courts routinely have been reluctant to prosecute rape and other crimes of sexual violence against black women, irrespective of the race of the accused.[8] Ultimately, black women have long been disregarded as "legitimate" victims due in part to sexually deviant stereotypes.

Depictions of black women as hypersexual were seen as provocation for being victimized by rape or sexual abuse. The invisible or nonexistent status of black women has led to the view that the violence they suffer is "obscured, routinized, and thereby legitimated."[9] Scathing evidence of this attitude toward black women is evident in the Philadelphia police department's failure to initiate investigations in more than 2,000 rape complaints from 1984 to 1997 because the police were skeptical of the victims and their moral character, especially when both the victim and assailant were African American.[10] The Philadelphia police sex crimes unit deliberately miscoded actual rape cases as 2701, indicating "investigation of the person" as opposed to an actual rape.[11] The majority of the victims in these "dumped" complaints were African American women.

The media's blatant disregard for minority victims of violence has reverberating consequences on a number of levels. First, it is clear that when society cares about victims of crime, and can empathize with their experience, the result is public outrage that has a catalytic effect on police response. The media are effective in stirring the sentiment of the public, which in turn increases police response and impacts the number of arrests, prosecutions, and convictions for violent crimes.[12] Second, the media have scrupulous power in making the unfortunate victim of a homicide's life meaningful when stories are replete with characteristics and details about the victim that commemorates them; this is comforting to family members reeling from their unspeakable and tragic loss. And finally, the act of murder is dehumanizing to the victim—media attention should make the focus of this reprehensible act about the *victim,* not a killer seeking infamy.

Thus, it is important to address the issue of selective media coverage of female victims of homicide for several reasons. First, the disparity in reporting the disappearance/homicides of female victims across racial categories is reflective of racial inequality and institutionalized racism in the social structure, both of which need to be addressed. The lack of reporting also reinforces this inequality. Second, news media are powerful instruments in conveying images that socially construct not only individuals' perceptions of crime and deviance,[13] but of victims as well.[14] The media's ability to persuade their audience by the way a story is presented has been referred to in the literature as "story framing". Story framing involves including characteristics and/or details in the reporting of events that provide the perceptual context that impacts public opinion. In other words, it shapes the opinion of the viewer or reader with regard to the victim. Third, and finally, the media, through the reporting of violent crimes, humanizes the victim and garners public sympathy for her while simultaneously generating outrage toward the offender; this results in increased pressure on law enforcement officials.[15]

Despite a widely held belief (at least in conversational discourse among people of color) that there is a bias in the media's coverage of crime, particularly in reference to minority victims, what is lacking in research are studies that illuminate racially biased reporting of homicides along the intersections of race and gender. Nevertheless, there are numerous studies that show how African Americans and Hispanics are overrepresented in the media as perpetrators of violent crime, but underrepresented as victims of violent crime.[16] With these factors in mind, let's begin with a discussion of the actual victimization rate of black women and what is portrayed in the mainstream media.

PROLOGUE

On March 27, 2013, I left my college office to head to Starbucks for a meeting that filled me with dread. I had prepared to sit down with the family of a high school friend, Michelle Jackson, who had been brutally raped and murdered on her way to school almost thirty years ago. I had often wondered what became of Michelle's devastated mother, Carlotta, whom I had not seen since Michelle's funeral in 1984. What caused me such anxiety was the fact that even though twenty-nine years had passed since my friend's murder, the pain was still raw and real to her family, and this was evident in the phone call I shared with Carlotta two nights before we met. Several weeks before our meeting at Starbucks, I discussed with students in my criminology course that I was in the process of writing a book about the role of race in media coverage of female homicide victims. During this discussion, I mentioned the murder of Michelle Jackson. One of my female students looked perplexed and abruptly left the room as I described some of the details of the homicide.

On the cold and snowy morning of January 24, 1984, my friend Michelle Kimberly Jackson, a sixteen-year-old student at Murray-Wright High School in Detroit, rose from her bed and began to get ready for school. Packing her book bag with texts and homework completed the night before, she said good-bye to her cousin Jodie Kenney and made her way to the bus

1

stop near the corner of Fenkell and Wildemere on the city's west side. It was approximately 6:45 A.M. during final exams week. Michelle, an honor student, wanted to be on time. She was an attractive and popular student who had recently moved in with her aunt to be closer to our high school and avoid the inconvenience of multiple bus rides to get to school. A neighbor on her way to work observed Michelle, a lone would-be passenger, in the dark and frigid dawn waiting at the bus stop at 7:05 A.M. Other than the killer, she was the last person to see Michelle alive.

A cloud of terror and anxiety hung in the air in Detroit that winter as a number of female students had been sexually assaulted en route to and from school. Approximately forty-seven girls had been raped between September 1983 and February 1984.[1] When the otherwise prompt and astute junior was not seen in class that day by her teachers and friends, and subsequently did not return home from school, Michelle's mother and cousin began to panic. Carlotta was quoted in the press as saying, "She just never did that . . . she always came home. When she didn't (come home) . . . I just knew something was wrong."[2] Family members made phone calls to Michelle's closest friends; we also became worried as each of us responded that we had not seen her that day either. By 9 P.M., the family filed a missing person's report with the Detroit police department. Early the next day, family members formed a search party and set out to find her. Retracing Michelle's steps in going from her home to the bus stop, Jodie Kenney and a male cousin separated from the group and walked in another direction, a short distance from the bus stop. They noticed a dilapidated garage located behind a row of abandoned buildings (and ironically only one block from Kenney's home), and instinctively decided to enter the structure. Lying in a corner of the garbage-strewn garage floor was Michelle's abused and lifeless body. The killer had strangled her with a pair of long johns she was wearing that morning and left her body nude from the waist down. She had been sexually assaulted, and as a final act of brutality, a dirty green soda bottle had been viciously shoved into her rectum.[3]

The violent and horrific nature of Michelle's death was not lost on me. She was one of my sister's closest friends at Murray-Wright High School, and my sisters and I rode the bus home with her almost daily after school. Even after so many years, I can still recall a shy and easily smiling girl with an enviable slender yet curvy figure and a mischievous giggle when something amused her. Her death struck a chord of fear and deep sadness within all of us who knew and loved her. It was my first realization that the capacity for human beings to inflict savagery on other human beings knows no bottom.

At the conclusion of my telling the class Michelle's story, the student returned to the classroom and sat silently for the duration of my lecture, and then tentatively approached me at the end of class to inform me that she knew Michelle's family. A tremendous feeling of incredulity washed over me as I thought about the many times I longed to find out how her mother had fared over the years. I told the student that I had wanted to speak with Michelle's mother to let her know that I was writing a book that would feature her daughter in the prologue; I did not want her blindsided by the information. I gave the student my contact information and was pleased when several weeks later, Carlotta agreed to speak with me and gave my student her number.

Nevertheless, I waited several days before I phoned Carlotta; I was at a loss as to how I would begin the conversation. I didn't want to compound her grief by revisiting the horror of Michelle's death. But there was also a deeply personal reason why I was less than sanguine to sit down with Michelle's mom. *Guilt.* Guilt that I wasn't the one snatched from a cold wintry bus stop that early January morning. Guilt that I wasn't the one who was viciously sexually violated and left in a lifeless heap on the filthy floor of a rotting and abandoned building. That guilt plagued all of Michelle's friends in the winter of 1984, and as this feeling came and went, guilt could not be avoided as our graduating class crossed the stage to receive our diplomas in June of that year. I was relieved that Carlotta was gracious and more than willing to speak with me. She notified me that she would come with Jodie and a few other relatives since they had been her support system over the years and that it would be difficult to discuss Michelle—despite all the years that had passed. A short time after we ended our conversation, my phone rang again, and it was Jodie Kenney. She told me that she would be accompanying Carlotta to our meeting and requested that I communicate directly with her (Jodie) if I needed additional information. "Carlotta does not do well after talking about Michelle. She wants to talk to you, but she will be in bed for three days afterwards. . . . The grief can get unbearable," Jodie explained. My heart sank at that revelation. I could only imagine the number of nights she would lie awake thinking about the suffering and terror her only daughter experienced that fateful morning.

When I arrived early at the coffeehouse that cold and gray afternoon, a smiling man who appeared to be in his late thirties greeted me. He asked if I was there to meet with Carlotta Jackson. He then took me to a table where she sat with another relative, nervously awaiting my arrival. Though she smiled at me warmly, her face wore the familiar mask of grief. My mother wore the same expression after my sister Suane (a year younger than I and one of Michelle's closest friends at Murray-Wright) suddenly died from a pulmonary embolism following a surgical procedure in 2007. "Nothing worse than losing a child," my mother said through tears almost daily since my sister's death.

Carlotta and I greeted each other with a hug, and she informed me that Jodie Kenney (Michelle's cousin and the unfortunate discoverer of her body) was running late to the meeting. She arrived minutes later and took a seat beside me, greeting me also with a warm embrace. As I began to tell them about the book I was in the process of writing, Jodie interrupted me and began to weep openly. She apologized and said, "I'm sorry . . . but when I look at you I can't help but wonder what Michelle would be like . . . would look like at your age." I was forty-seven years old at the time, and I, too, wondered about the very the same thing. It was painfully obvious that no matter how many years had transpired between now and Michelle's death nearly thirty years ago, there was no closure for this family. How many times had Jodie and Carlotta looked at women in their forties and wondered the same thing Jodie confessed to me? Who would Michelle be today? Would she have become a lawyer? A doctor? Or perhaps chosen academia as I had? Would she be married? How many children would she have borne? The inquiry was tragic.

There were a number of profoundly disturbing details that emerged from our discussion that were unknown to me, and I was deeply disturbed by them. Carlotta and Jodie told me that the police were reluctant to file a missing person's report on Michelle, suggesting that she was a runaway. The family strongly protested this assertion and angrily stressed that Michelle was an honor student. They insisted that her disappearance was completely contrary to her character. At one point, in frustration, one officer snapped at Carlotta that if she wasn't satisfied with their response, she and her family could "look for her yourself!" Horrifically, they did just that and found her raped and strangled body in an abandoned garage. That same officer, with an ashamed and contrite expression, had to drive an emotionally shattered Carlotta Jackson home from the crime scene.

Unfortunately, to date, Michelle's murder remains unsolved. Police arrested and a jury convicted a suspect named Eddie Joe Lloyd for Michelle's rape and murder. However, seventeen years later, the Innocence Project, through DNA testing, exonerated Lloyd of the charges, and he was freed from prison. It was determined the Detroit police homicide investigators coerced a confession from Lloyd, a man suffering from schizophrenia who developed an interest in the case from reading newspaper articles on the homicide.[4]

Despite the sadness of the occasion, our conversation that day renewed hope in Michelle's family that this book could possibly reopen the investigation into her death and possibly lead to finding her killer. To say that that Michelle's family was desperate for any help they could get solving her murder would be a gross understatement. The release of Eddie Joe Lloyd from prison seemed to revictimize the family as it completely destroyed their trust in law enforcement. Worse, it made them feel as though Michelle's life had no value and that her death was of no consequence. In short, Michelle was one of many invisible victims—African American women who have been slain and are ignored by both the media and law enforcement. These cases often go unsolved, leaving the victims' loved ones in a perpetual state of shock, grief, and anguish.

Without question, my friend's brutal rape and murder is one of many tragic stories of violence perpetrated against women every day in this country. Crimes of this nature evoke fear, outrage, disgust, and, oftentimes, a demand for swift and severe punishment for the perpetrator. However, the public's reaction to violent crimes against women is contingent upon media coverage, and without it, societal pressure on law enforcement to solve these crimes is minimal at most or nonexistent at worst. Most disturbingly, the public's reaction to violent crimes against women is also predicated upon society's *view* of the victim, or specifically whether the victim is seen as deserving of sympathy and outrage or not.

Even at eighteen years of age, I was taken aback at the lack of outcry from the community, press, and law enforcement for justice in Michelle's brutal murder. The press documented that at that time the citizens of Detroit were up in arms about the continual rapes of teens en route to school and that one of these rapes eventually culminated in a vicious homicide, yet they provided little attention to Michelle as a *victim*. It was as though she was simply an appendage to an increasing number of schoolgirl rape victims who served as an unfortunate indication that these unspeakable crimes had now escalated to murder. The scant coverage of her death failed miserably at portraying a sweet and academically ambitious young woman who is forever lost to her family and friends.

The purpose of this book is to examine the bias in the mainstream media's reporting of homicides of female victims of color, and law enforcement's culpability in its own failure at times to thoroughly and aggressively investigate these deaths. A further goal for this book is to ignite a discussion of one of the most insidious ways that this form of discrimination harms African Americans—by obscuring the stories of victims whose voices have been forever silenced by murder. In doing so, the media devalues these victims (like Michelle), ignores their humanity, and minimizes how they (as much as white female victims) are irreplaceable in the lives of the people who loved them. This book will attempt to speak for them.

CHAPTER 1

BLACK WOMEN AS
HOMICIDE VICTIMS

Reality vs. Media Representation

SEVERAL YEARS AGO WHILE SURFING THROUGH CABLE TELEVISION channels for something of interest to watch, I happened upon the *Nancy Grace* program on CNN. Grace, a former Los Angeles prosecutor, is known for her brash and aggressive approach in examining crimes against society's most vulnerable victims, namely women and children as victims of homicide. That night's program centered on a young white wife and mother from North Carolina who had been brutally bludgeoned to death in her home as her young child slept in a nearby room. In her customary style, Grace was seething with anger and berating defense attorneys on the show's panel of guest commentators who dared to proffer a possible defense for the victim's husband, the suspected killer. At the time that the show aired, I was in the process of defending my dissertation proposal on the topic of the media's coverage of female homicide victims by race.

Being drawn to programs such as the *Nancy Grace* show was not unusual for me since I have held a lifelong interest in issues related to violence against women. Needless to say, I was impressed with Nancy Grace's passion and vigilance in addressing a problem that is all too often ignored or minimized within the United States and globally. Intimate partner violence remains the leading cause of death for women ages fifteen to forty-four. Nonetheless, women are less likely to be victims of violence than men.[1] Yet while homicides in particular have declined overall, what has not changed is the fact that women are far more often murdered by men than men are by women. Essentially, even with declining homicide rates in the United States, the violent deaths of women continue to be fodder for increased ratings on television news programs; yet not all victims are viewed as rating bonanzas.

As I continued to tune in to Nancy Grace's program, I became acutely aware that she almost exclusively covered violent deaths of white female victims. If the basis of the show's coverage was to highlight shocking or appalling crimes against women and children, statistics would indicate that black women were far more likely to be victims of homicide. Reviewing FBI data from 1997, black women were almost four times more likely than white women to be homicide victims:

- Black females had a 1 in 232 chance of being a homicide victim.
- White females had a 1 in 905 chance of being a homicide victim.[2]

Table 1 indicates:

- Black females are almost two-and-a-half times more likely to be a homicide victim than white females.
- Black males are more than six-and-a-half times more likely to be a homicide victim than white males.
- White females are least likely to be a homicide victim compared to any of the three other cited groups.

Despite the fact that the population of black females in the United States in 2011 was 22 million compared to 100 million white females, they are

Table 1. 2011 Homicides in the United States by Race and Sex

	*Population**	*Homicides by Group*[†]	*Rate per 100,000*
White Males	97,166,000	4,079	4.2
Black Males	19,489,000	5,416	27.8
White Females	100,256,000	1,745	1.7
Black Females	22,088,000	910	4.1

*Data retrieved from U.S. Census Data, 2011.

[†]Data retrieved from FBI Uniform Crime Reports.

more at risk for lethal violence. They are also less likely to be informed of this unsettling reality by the media.

So, what is the probable impact of crimes against black women being underrepresented in the media when the reality is that they are more likely to be victims of homicide than their white counterparts? Unsurprisingly, it is a false sense of security in the face of very real and grave danger. Some black and Latina women living in New York City interviewed by researchers regarding the effects of media and images of crime victims indicated that they had less fear of crime because they falsely believed white women to be the more common victims of homicides based on the extensive and continuous media coverage of white female victims.[3] Further, they viewed white women as "ideal" victims who were submissive, weaker than ethnic women, and unable to protect themselves from crime. In essence, the media contributed to the perpetuation of viewing white women as primary victims, particularly in homicides perpetrated by strangers.

Most striking is that these women of color also believed that for them to be recognized as victims worthy of media coverage, it had to be demonstrated that they were better than the perceived stereotypes of their racial group—in other words, that they were good mothers, were students or in college, were religious, and so forth. It is clear to many African American women that they are at the bottom of the list when it comes to news coverage—even regarding homicides. As an African American woman myself, it does not escape my attention when news outlets eagerly provide extensive coverage of missing and/or murdered white women, while simultaneously black females are also disappearing or being murdered and have received little to no attention from the media.

Recent statistics on crime trends indicate that violent crime in the United States has been decreasing since 2005. In that year, there were 16,740 homicides in the United States. By 2011, there were 14,612 murders, reflecting a decline of 12.7 percent.[4] However, in large urban areas, African Americans have continued to be victims of homicide at an alarming rate. In Detroit, in the year 2012 alone there were at least 400 homicides, while in Chicago there were 500 murders in the same year (most of which came from the largely black neighborhood of Englewood).[5] It stands to reason that regardless of declining national crime trends, the reality for minorities living in low socioeconomic communities is that violent death is an everyday occurrence whether the news outlets substantiate this or not. In fact, while researching literature on the topic of media coverage of crime and the general public's view of crime victims, I was taken aback at the question posed in the abstract of one such article: "Why has the public persisted in believing that violent crime is a widespread national problem in the U.S. despite declining trends in crime and the fact that crime is concentrated in urban locations?" The implication of this question was not lost on me either as an African American or as a sociologist. It is clear that the "public" the author was referring to was middle class and white, since this group is less likely to live in an urban community, where occurrences of violent crime tend to outpace those on a national level. Therefore, the author suggests that this "public" should be less concerned about violent crime when it is not part of their community and thus is not their problem. This attitude forms the crux of this book, specifically that victimization of white females is seen by a biased media and public as representative of a threat to *all women*. But if violence happens to black females in urban communities, most white females need not fear for their own personal safety.

Given that violent crime is on the increase in urban and poor neighborhoods, it is both interesting and demoralizing that these statistical facts tend to be ignored by the mainstream media time and time again when it comes to crime victims of color. So common was the extensive media coverage of white female victims that a term was dubbed to label the phenomenon—"Missing White Girl Syndrome"[6]—and numerous blogs and Internet websites have discussed the issue of disproportionate media coverage for these particular victims.[7] In contrast, despite the fact that African American females (as per table 1) are 2.4 times more likely than white females to be victims of homicide, their deaths are not frequently reported in the press. In some cases, when the murder of inner-city women of color does get media attention, many reporters provide negative background details about the victim, implying that she was somehow culpable, particularly if there was a history of substance abuse, prostitution, or sexual promiscuity.[8] One can assume that even the suggestion of sexually liberal behavior can be enough to negatively shape the image of the victim in the public's eye, especially if she is a minority.

This pattern was evident in the reporting of a recent homicide of two black women in the city of Hamtramck, Michigan, an urban and ethnically diverse community that borders Detroit. On February 28, 2012, twenty-two-year-old Ashley Conaway and her best friend, eighteen-year-old Abreeya Brown, were kidnapped by gunpoint from Brown's stepfather's home in Hamtramck. Approximately one month later, on March 25, 2012, Ashley and Abreeya were found in a shallow grave after being bound, gagged, and shot at close range in the back of the head.[9]

The suspected motive behind the killings was that after spending the evening together at a strip club on February 8, 2012 (a detail provided by the Fox 2 Detroit news program), Conaway was shot at by one of the alleged perpetrators after she rebuffed his attempts to have a romantic relationship with her, and then subsequently refused to accept a proposed bribe of $5,000 from the assailant in lieu of testifying against him for the assault.[10] The news reporter may not have conveyed the fact that the two young women spent an evening at a strip club with their suspected killers to intentionally discredit the victims or somehow imply that their moral character was questionable. However, this is often the inevitable impact of such a disclosure. The press initially reported that both victims were college students and had no prior criminal records, yet some might question their moral aptitude when positive elements of their background are contrasted with evenings out with ex-cons at "gentlemen's" clubs. Details such as these lead to the questioning of the woman's character and make it difficult for the public to sympathize with the victim; it might lead viewers to believe that she does not deserve the coverage.

Numerous scholars have written about the impact of the media on how society views various issues.[11] For the most part, the way journalists "frame" the stories they report shapes the media's influence, thereby setting the context of the story for the reader or viewer. Again, the description of a victim and the facts of the case can elicit empathy and moral outrage or an apathetic dismissal by the reader or viewer that the victim "put herself in that position," especially when there was a relationship between the female victim and the male perpetrator and there is a history of violence between them.[12] For example, the story might mention family members' concerns about the victim's relationship with the abuser, their efforts to protect her from the abuse, and the victim's refusal to terminate the relationship. On July 2, 2012, thirty-three-year-old Shawanda Spratling, of Detroit, was fatally beaten and shot by her ex-boyfriend, thirty-five-year-old Larry Crawford, whom she began (according to the news article) secretly dating after he was recently released from prison. The story referenced her father's objection to the relationship and his warnings to his daughter to end the relationship. "It must've been 10 years ago—I chased him out of this house myself!" her grief-stricken father told the press.[13] One must wonder how many readers would be inclined to have less sympathy for the victim under such circumstances—her father tried in vain to protect her, she defied his advice and secretly continued the relationship, and the killer had a past violent and threatening history with the victim.

On the other hand, the power of the media also lies in their vital role in naming a social problem and acting as a catalyst in the construction of viable solutions.[14] In short, the media's "framing" of a social problem (in this case, the murder of black and white women) determines society's response. If the victim is portrayed as undeserving of the violence perpetrated against her, and is attractive, relatable, and likable, the public is more inclined to empathize with the victim and be moved to action on her behalf. Law enforcement is called upon to solve the homicide. Without public sympathy for victims of domestic violence, it is unlikely that legislation will be enacted to address this issue as a social problem.[15] Here, I contrast six cases of homicides of black and white women to illustrate the apparent bias in the media's determination of which victims receive prominent coverage and, consequently, which cases police determine to investigate vigorously.

The race of the victim determines whether a murder receives prominent coverage by newspapers or other media outlets. The media are quick to dismiss this assertion, and instead claim that stories that get attention are those that are unusual, are rare, or provoke outrage from the general public.[16] When one observes the crime stories that fit these criteria, however, the focus tends to be on those with white victims. To illustrate, I am reminded of a case that occurred in Michigan in 2012. On January 25, 2012, fifty-six-year-old Jane Bashara was found strangled in the backseat of her car in an alley on the east side of Detroit. The white and upper-middle-class Grosse Pointe mother of two and successful businesswoman was reported missing by her husband, Bob Bashara, after she failed to return home from work. Joseph Gentz, a handyman who worked for the Bashara family, readily confessed to the murder shortly after Jane's body was found. He then implicated Bob Bashara in the homicide as the person who paid him to strangle Jane in their Grosse Pointe home, and instructed Gentz to leave the body in her Mercedes SUV in Detroit to give the appearance that the victim was killed as a result of an attempted robbery or carjacking.[17] Prosecutors have charged Bob Bashara with first-degree murder in the killing of his wife, and he is facing additional charges of attempting to hire a hit man to kill Joseph Gentz, among other acts of witness tampering.

During the murder investigation into Jane's death, there were a number of lewd details that emerged regarding the background of Bob Bashara—from his illicit love affairs with a mistress and other women, to his secret sex dungeon in the basement of one of his commercial property buildings, as well as his belonging to a sadomasochistic website.[18]

However, even before these details were uncovered and disclosed to the public, the extent of local and national media coverage in this case eclipsed any other homicide that occurred in Detroit or its surrounding suburbs for the entire year. The murder of Jane Bashara was featured on *ABC Nightly News*, the Huffington Post, and *Good Morning America*.

On NBC's *Dateline* evening news program, the story about the Bashara homicide was titled "Secrets in the Suburbs," and the narrator referenced the idyllic and prosperous community of Grosse Pointe several times during the news clip.[19]

In contrast, there were 387 homicides in Detroit in 2012, with the majority of the victims being male. Among the victims, forty-three were female (four of these victims were white females), and only a few of these victims received at least one article in the local newspapers about their deaths. The Wayne County medical examiner's office for the city of Detroit noted that there were six homicides of black females during the month of January 2012 (in addition to the Jane Bashara homicide), and of those, I found that only three victims received press coverage (albeit it local) of their murders. Twenty-one-year-old Claudia Benson, a nursing student, was robbed of her purse and gunned down after leaving a local bar and grill with friends. What seemed to bring the story to the attention of the press was that at the arraignment of the accused shooter, thirty-five-year-old Jacob Welcome Wells, the defendant's family attempted to physically assault Benson's family as they left the courthouse.[20]

In another case, twelve-year-old Kade'jah Davis was shot multiple times through the door of her home when the accused assailant, nineteen-year-old Joshua Brown, argued with the victim's mother over a missing or stolen cell phone. When Kade'jah's mother closed the door on the defendant, he fired shots into the home, and Kade'jah Davis was struck several times while doing homework in her living room. Again, another shocking detail of the case that seemed to make the story "newsworthy" was that the defendant's thirty-five-year-old mother actually drove him to and from the murder scene![21]

The third black female victim who was murdered in the month of January and received coverage from the local press was twenty-year-old Tailar Davis, who was shot execution style in the back of the head along with her boyfriend while they sat in the front seat of a vehicle. It was reported in the press that the victim was a shy nursing student who, while in high school, turned down the opportunity to speak at her high school graduation as valedictorian because she was too afraid to speak in front of an audience.[22] To date, the Tailar Davis murder case remains unsolved; the lone article on this case focused on the mothers of the two victims seeking the public's help in finding the killer.

Certainly, Jane Bashara is not the first woman to die at the hands of her husband, and beyond her education and socioeconomic class, she is yet another unfortunate victim of domestic homicide. Both Tailar Davis and Claudia Benson were young, attractive, and motivated women pursuing careers in nursing, and Kade'jah Davis was not yet a teen who had a 4.0 GPA, loved school, and was adored by her friends, teachers, and especially her family. Yet none of these victims received continuous primetime coverage by the media as in the Bashara case. Most heartbreaking was a statement made by Kade'jah's grieving ten-year old male cousin to reporters. "She would always play with me. She always got me," he said. "She always understood me."[23]

When news outlets decide to give priority to homicide stories, there are a number of factors that determine whether the story receives prominent coverage—for example, homicides with multiple victims, black suspects, female suspects, white victims, and female victims (who were most often white).[24] However, there appears to be no explication for the differences in coverage of female homicides between racial groups. Criminal justice professor and researcher Derek J. Paulsen found that female victims murdered by male assailants had longer articles (greater word count) compared to male victim/male assailant homicides since female homicides were viewed as statistical anomalies (yet again, he failed to investigate whether this prominence is less pronounced when the victim is a black female).[25]

The media acknowledge that the public tends to show a keen interest in homicides when the victim is female (just look how often true crime documentaries feature female victims compared to males), and within these news articles or televised coverage, there tends to be more information about the victim's background and her value to her family and/or community; even the details of the homicide seems to border on the salacious and sensational.[26] Again, the rarity of certain specific types of victims is also an indication of which homicides receive "breaking news" coverage by the media—murders involving Asian or Asian American victims, females, and multiple-victim homicides—and thus these stories are not only more apt to be more lengthy, but they are more often located in the front section or conspicuous sections of the newspaper.[27] Here the story catches the reader's attention, and the impact of this awareness is immediate. Moving the public either to action or anger, it is the hope of victims' families that humanizing their loved ones and showcasing details of the killing may generate additional tips to solve the crime and/or increase pressure on law enforcement to bring the perpetrator(s) to justice. In contrast, crime briefs or shorter crime columns are most likely to feature homicides considered to be "statistically common," such as blacks and Hispanics as victims, male victim homicides, and murders with a single victim.[28] Equally troubling is that the prevalence of racial stereotypes of blacks as criminals (as opposed to being victims) results in the public being not only less sympathetic to black homicide victims but more likely indifferent as well.

CHAPTER 2

THE DESERVING VS. UNDESERVING VICTIM

Case Studies of Biased Media Reporting and Law Enforcement Intervention

ONE UNSETTLING REALITY ABOUT SOCIETY'S VIEW OF CRIME VICTIMS is that there are times when victims are blamed for the violence committed against them. Perceptions of undeserving (the victim did not deserve or provoke his or her death) or deserving (the victim asked for it) victims of violence[1] are a consequence of the media constructing victim culpability in the manner in which they cover news stories.[2] In such cases, negative publicity about a crime victim may engender victim blame. The psychologist Melvin Lerner has argued that individuals who believe in a "just world" (or essentially that both bad and good things happen for a reason) may directly or indirectly attribute blame to crime victims if the framing of the story suggests the victim was culpable to some extent.[3] For example, details about a rape victim being intoxicated or leaving a party at 2 A.M. can lead some to believe the victim in some way deserved the assault. After all, a person might reason, "Why would a decent woman be out so late knowing that the world is a dangerous place?" The media have the power to counteract victim blaming in the manner that they "frame" the person. Isabel Correia and her colleagues examined "secondary victimization" and found that the assignment of positive characteristics to victims of violent crime increased the study participants' tendency to empathize with the victims and to view them as undeserving of the violence they suffered.[4] The authors describe secondary victimization as the process by which victims of violence experience feelings of being revictimized by negative or harsh judgmental attitudes from others. This type of victimization can also occur in the manner in which law enforcement officers handle sexual assault complaints from victims.[5]

Additionally, when newspapers provide additional descriptive or personal information about a murder victim, it adds a layer of empathy to the story and causes readers to feel greater compassion for the victim and the victim's family and friends.[6] Research has indicated that the public's resonance with the victim as a result of media attention has even shaped the outcome of criminal proceedings in court. Gary Moran and Brian Cutler reported in their study of pretrial publicity and jurors that when potential jurors read stories in the newspapers about the victim's personal characteristics and about the effect the homicide had on the victim's family, they were more likely to believe that the accused was actually guilty of the crime.[7]

One primary way news stories humanize the victim to the public is their inclusion of personal photographs of the victim. More than sixty years ago, this assertion was supported by the sociologist James Davis, who in his 1952 study of reports on crime in Colorado newspapers concluded that photographs were an important part of a story since the public tends to be "influenced by them considerably," primarily because photographs make the death of the victim seem more palpable.[8] In essence, when victims are portrayed in the press as individuals who made a contribution to others or mattered to those who loved them, the public is more likely to perceive that person as undeserving of his or her violent death and to demand that punishment be rendered against the perpetrator(s). When the press portray victims as people who matter, they, in turn, matter to the public.

In this text I present a number of cases that illustrate a pattern of mainstream media's and law enforcement's discounting of black female victims of homicide. The purpose in doing so is not to be salacious with details about very brutal murders of women, but to elucidate this social problem with qualitative information that makes the issue tangible to the reader. It is important to note the symbiotic connection between media coverage and the response of law enforcement—one reinforces the other. Victims who garner prominent media coverage tend to have crimes against them investigated more vigorously than do victims whose crimes have scant reporting in newspapers and/or on evening news programs. The substantiation of the interdependence of media and police response will be evident in the case studies presented in this chapter.

ONE CITY, TWO TALES: THE CASE OF ROMONA MOORE (BLACK) AND SVETLANA ARONOV (WHITE) (2003)

On the late spring evening of April 24, 2003, Romona Moore's mother, Elle Carmichael, was getting worried. It was past 10 P.M., and she had not heard from her honor student daughter since 7 P.M., the time Romona left her Flatbush home in Brooklyn, New York, to meet a friend at Burger King. Even though Romona was twenty-one years of age, the shy and reticent African American young woman seemed much younger than her age and was very serious about her studies at Hunter College. Therefore, it was unlike her to be out later than promised. She had only a few close friends and no boyfriend—factors that further entrenched her mother's concern. Nevertheless, Elle Carmichael reassured herself that Romona was fine and turned in for the night, telling herself that perhaps her daughter, at twenty-one years of age, was exercising independence for the first time.

However, at nine o'clock the next morning, when Romona had not yet returned home, her mother immediately contacted the police. After calling 911, she waited anxiously for officers to arrive at her home to take a report about her missing daughter. When two New York Police Department (NYPD) officers arrived at the Carmichael residence thirty minutes later, they were less than sympathetic toward the frantic mother. While she assured them repeatedly that Romona's absence was completely out of character and divulged that her daughter was an honor student and homebody, the police officers thought it necessary to repeatedly "remind" Elle Carmichael that her daughter was an adult, and typically in such cases, law enforcement does not consider the situation to be that of a missing and endangered person. "Maybe she has a boyfriend she didn't want to tell you about," one of the officers offered cynically. Elle emphatically disagreed and begged the officers to take a report to investigate her daughter's disappearance. Taking pity on the nearly hysterical mother, the officers reluctantly completed a complaint form regarding Romona Moore. As is customary in missing person cases, the officers informed Elle that if she had not heard from her daughter by seven o'clock that evening, she should contact the precinct and let them know that Romona had been missing a full twenty-four hours. At 7 P.M. there was still no sign of Romona, and her mother immediately called the station. The reception she received was terse and scolding. According to the grieving mother, a detective snapped, "Lady, why are you calling here? Your daughter is 21! These officers never should have taken the report in the first place."[9] The following day, Elle Carmichael's missing person's complaint regarding Romona was closed.[10]

Tragically, the case was not "closed"; Romona Moore's brutal rape and murder were commencing only blocks away from her family home. While police officers debated the merit of investigating Romona's disappearance, the young woman was being held in a dungeon of horrors and enduring sexual assault, torture, and sadistic beatings over the course of several days. Elle Carmichael could not have imagined then that her beloved daughter was being held captive and subjected to vicious rapes and beatings, but she knew her child well enough to know that Romona was in grave danger. As days passed and she became even more frustrated with the indifferent and apathetic response from law enforcement, the determined mother and other family members created missing person posters with Romona's picture on them and distributed them throughout their neighborhood. Although the officers did not articulate what Elle Carmichael felt viscerally, she believed the inactivity from investigators was due in large part to race. "I don't see any other reason but race and class. . . . If this was a white kid, they would never had done this. I had to say to the detectives one day: 'You know, I feel the same emotions and pain as a white person.'"[11] Apparently, a federal court judge in Brooklyn agreed with Carmichael and ruled in 2008 that the Romona Moore murder case be reopened to investigate racial bias in missing person cases in New York. This also allowed Carmichael to file a civil rights lawsuit against the NYPD, charging the police with discrimination in the way cases of missing African Americans are handled compared to those of whites. Another family member echoed Elle Carmichael's sentiment in an interview with the press. "We were handled with contempt by the police," he said. "We kept pleading with them; she's not that type of girl."[12]

The statement "not that kind of girl" implies that Romona Moore's moral character was called into question by investigators, and this unfortunately reflects a normative pattern of historical racial stereotypes about black female sexuality. The sociologist Rupe Simms used the term "Jezebel" to describe the century-old stereotype of black females as sexually promiscuous and insatiable in their quest to seduce men, thereby resolving the cognitive dissonance of white males who routinely raped black slave women with impunity.[13] Furthermore, the promotion of the sexual stereotype of black women benefited the slave trade, as the proliferation of their reproduction was crucial to slave traders' economic interests. Black women's supposed voracious sexual appetites made it necessary that they not only "mate" with male slaves but also that their white masters were "duty bound" to impregnate them as well to increase their chattel.[14] The political scientist and journalist Melissa Harris-Perry has noted that the historical view of black women as lewd and promiscuous denied them the right to be seen as legitimate victims of sexual assault. "Under such conditions, black women—promiscuous by definition—found it nearly impossible to convince the legal establishment that men of any race should be prosecuted for sexually assaulting them. The rape of black women is simply no crime at all."[15]

Even today this belief about the immoral nature of black women is ubiquitous in the media and shapes the response of law enforcement in cases of sexual assault and other crimes of violence against black females. In 2008, Toni Irving conducted a study of the Philadelphia police department's refusal to investigate more than 2,000 cases of rape between 1984 and 1997, where most of the victims were African Americans. Her study provided empirical support that the police department's egregious neglect in investigating these crimes was shaped in large part by law enforcement's deeply ingrained beliefs that black women were culpable in their alleged victimization because of their promiscuity. Rather than pursue the perpetrator, officers labeled the complaint as an "investigation of the person" to suggest that the victim was not being forthcoming in her accusation of rape.[16] Tragically, the Philadelphia police department's failure to investigate these rapes was the basis a lawsuit by the family of murder victim Shannon Schieber, who was raped and strangled to death by a serial rapist, twenty-nine-year-old Troy Graves. A federal grand jury cleared the city and the Philadelphia police department from liability in Schieber's murder, despite the fact that Graves's DNA matched at least five of the rape cases that the sex crimes unit did not investigate.[17]

Numerous other studies confirmed that the social location of women of color serves as an impediment in law enforcement's response to violence against them, thereby contributing to both their increasing vulnerability and subsequent invisibility as victims.[18] As such, it is not unusual for female victims of color or their families to attest to their good moral character while imploring law enforcement to investigate crimes against them.[19]

On May 6, 2003, Elle Carmichael's worst fear was realized when the body of her daughter was discovered. Romona Moore's death was not immediate. According to police sources, the accused killers, Troy Hendrix and Kayson Pearson, brought at least two friends to the basement of the apartment where they were keeping her hostage to show off their gruesome treatment of her. One such witness, Rolando Jack, even spoke with the teary, frightened, and brutalized young woman as she was forced by her kidnappers to recount in detail what happened to her after they pulled her off the street and dragged her into the basement apartment, where she shortly thereafter met her death.[20] Incredibly, instead of immediately notifying the police of the horrors he witnessed and getting help, Jack left the basement and went to a family baby shower in Maryland. He claimed he was afraid of the two violent sociopaths and feared for his life if he went to the police.[21] Had he contacted police to tell them of Romona's fate, it is possible that she could have been saved.

Facts indicate that within days of that encounter, Hendrix and Pearson bludgeoned her to death, wrapped her nude body in a sheet, and dumped her body under an abandoned ice cream truck only blocks from her home. The killers crushed her skull as well as the bones in her face, and they burned her body with cigarettes. The cuts and gruesome wounds to her body served as evidence of the torture she endured (the killers even cut the webbing between her fingers). Again, the police were of no use in discovering her tragic end—someone made an anonymous phone call to the Carmichael home to alert them to the whereabouts of Romona's body, and the family went to the location and waited for police to arrive to find her.[22] The devastating details of the honor student's murder is compounded by the helplessness and frustration faced by her family. In her desperation to find her daughter, Elle Carmichael reached out to the media to broadcast Romona's disappearance and again hit a roadblock. No reporter was interested in covering the story.[23]

Ironically, even her sociopathic killers followed the news, eager to see if the newspapers or evening news programs would cover the story. Shortly after murdering and then dumping Romona's body, Hendrix and Pearson kidnapped and raped a fifteen-year-old girl and held her captive in the same basement where they tortured and murdered Romona. Before their young victim bravely escaped her sleeping captors by licking the duct tape that covered her mouth until it loosened and then chewed through the tape that bound her wrists, she overhead the killers complaining that news reporters weren't talking about Romona's disappearance.[24]

In a missing person's case that occurred a month before the Romona Moore kidnap-slaying, the police and media response was anything but non-existent. In Dickensian fashion, one could observe a "tale of two cities" in comparing the media's coverage and the expeditious response of law enforcement in the disappearance of Svetlana Aronov. The forty-four-year-old white wife of an internist physician and mother of two was also a rare book dealer and lived in Upper Manhattan. According to media accounts, on March 3, 2003, at 2:30 P.M., Svetlana Aronov left her apartment building with her father's cocker spaniel in tow (she was dog sitting for him while he was out of town) to go for a walk after speaking with her husband on the phone. Her husband stated that she called to remind him to come directly home from work after 7 P.M. to relieve his stepmother from babysitting their nine-year-old daughter after school, and that Svetlana promised to leave the keys to their apartment with the doorman for his stepmother to gain entry.[25] Additionally, Svetlana was supposed to pick her father up from the airport by five o'clock that afternoon. When her husband's stepmother arrived with the couple's young daughter at the apartment to get the keys from the doorman, she was informed that Svetlana never left the keys as promised. Nor did she arrive at the airport to pick up her father, who waited anxiously for a couple of hours before finally catching a cab to the Aronovs' apartment, where he waited in the lobby of the building.

Before leaving work, Dr. Alexander Aronov received a call from his stepmother, who told him that she took his daughter to her home in Queens since no keys were left for them to get into the apartment. He then left work, retrieved his daughter, and returned home, only to be startled by news from his father-in-law that Svetlana never picked him up from the airport and that she did not answer her cell phone during the numerous attempts to contact her. By this time it was 10 P.M., and her husband was very worried and called the police. By 10:30, officers arrived at the Aronovs' apartment and took a missing person's report from Svetlana's husband and collected recent pictures of her to conduct a neighborhood search.[26] At least two-dozen officers were assigned to the search, and police tracking dogs were also used to track the scent of the missing woman as well as that of the cocker spaniel, Bim.

In stark dissimilarity to Romona Moore's disappearance, the *New York Times* reported that "police department crime stopper vans crawled up and down York Avenue yesterday [March 5—*two days* after she was reported missing] trumpeting word of her disappearance and trolling for tips."[27] Local news outlets picked up the story the following day, and by March 5,

2003, the first of many newspaper articles began to appear announcing Svetlana Aronov's disappearance. For one week straight the *New York Times* published stories almost daily, updating the public on the case. By April, even *People* magazine featured a story about the missing rare book dealer.[28] On May 6, 2003, several months after her disappearance, Aronov's body was spotted floating in the river, near a pier on the Queens side of the East River. The following day, the body of a small dog matching the cocker spaniel's description washed ashore near the Throgs Neck Bridge.[29] To date, it is unclear whether Aronov was murdered or committed suicide; there have been no arrests made in the case.

The immediacy of the police response was not lost on Romona Moore's family. "They handled the dog better than my niece's disappearance," commented Romona's uncle, Patrick Patterson. He also attributed the apparent discriminatory treatment by law enforcement to class. "But I guess we don't probably pay enough taxes like everybody else."[30] Not surprisingly, the NYPD denied that either race or class was a factor in the manner in which both cases were investigated. Instead, the urgency in commencing with an immediate search for Svetlana Aronov was attributed to "red flags."[31] Specifically, the aspects of the case that warranted an abrupt reaction by law enforcement was that Aronov only took keys and her cell phone with her; the missing woman had specified plans to pick up her father from the airport and leave keys to her apartment with the doorman; and, most notably, she was very excited about an upcoming twenty-fifth wedding anniversary ski trip. Michael P. O'Looney, the police department's spokesperson, stated that the circumstances were different in both cases, emphasizing that young adults such as Moore are more likely to disappear voluntarily and then resurface days later.[32] Perhaps this explains why the police remained steadfast in their assessment that her disappearance did not warrant a full-fledged search comparable to that for Svetlana Aronov, despite the arrant protests of her family that Romona "was not that kind of girl."

The *New York Times* claimed that the police had not alerted the paper to the disappearance of Romona Moore; therefore stories about her being missing were not featured in the *Times*. After her death, the media began to

25

report in earnest the dissatisfaction her family had with the police response, suggesting that more vigilance on the part of the officers could have possibly saved Moore's life. However, Sean Gardiner, a reporter for the *Village Voice* in New York City who wrote the most explicit and detailed article on Moore's murder, stated that Elle Carmichael reached out to the media about her missing daughter, but "no reporter showed interest in the story."[33] It was not until Moore's family incessantly called local politicians (who in turn pressured the precinct to reopen the case for investigation) that action was taken on the young woman's disappearance, albeit too late to avert her brutal death.

Yet police were notably more expedient in reaching out to newspapers and local news stations to broadcast Aronov's disappearance; the *New York Times* provided almost daily coverage until her body was found almost two months after she disappeared. As stated previously, even a major national publication with widespread readership (*People* magazine) throughout the United States provided a story on Aronov's disappearance. Clearly, it is not only the media that determine which victims are worthy of prominent coverage—law enforcement is also selective about which victims are *worthy* of amplified efforts to bring justice.

On August 4, 2014, federal judge Nina Gershon dismissed Elle Carmichael's lawsuit against the NYPD, claiming that Romona's mother failed to demonstrate a consistent and persistent pattern of racial bias in the police department's investigation of missing persons' reports. While Judge Gershon acknowledged that there was obvious "differing treatment" between the Moore and Aronov cases, she did not observe evidence of "a practice so persistent and widespread as to constitute the existence of a widespread practice."[34] Regardless of whether Elle Carmichael provided enough evidence to support her claim against the police department for their failure to act in an urgent manner in looking for Romona, as was the case in Aronov's disappearance, the federal court's dismissal of her lawsuit must have wielded a devastating blow. She lost a daughter to a murder so brutal and tragic that it defies most people's ability to comprehend the mind and motive of Romona's killers, and now she has lost her opportunity to hold law enforcement accountable for their lack of due diligence in fulfilling their oath to serve and protect.

LITTLE GIRL LOST . . . AND FOUND: THE CASE OF ALICIA CHANTA MOORE (BLACK) (2012) AND HAYLIE WHITE (WHITE) (2013)

For most parents, waiting for a child to arrive home from school is uneventful. From the time the bus arrives at the stop until the time a student bounces through the door in search of a quick snack or a break from academics, the pattern is routine enough to set a clock by. So one can only imagine the anxiety that the mother of sixteen-year-old Alicia Chanta Moore (no relation to Romona) felt as hours passed and her daughter had not yet returned from school on November 6, 2012. The teen, described by family members as quiet and shy, was last seen exiting her school bus at 3:25 P.M. by the driver and via security cameras. This was the last image of her being seen alive.[35] Tragically, her battered body was found on November 12, 2012, at noon in a trunk along a Greenville, Texas, highway by construction workers.

On the day Alicia went missing at least three hours passed and the young girl had not returned home from school, prompting her mother to telephone the police for assistance. What happened next remains an ongoing controversy and point of contention between the African American community in Greenville and the city's police department. According to numerous media reports, the family demanded that an Amber Alert be issued for a statewide and countywide search for Alicia, but for reasons yet to satisfy the murdered girl's family, none was issued.[36] In cases where an Amber Alert is ordered by authorities, a search for a missing child or young person begins immediately. Local television news stations broadcast a physical description of the child and details of his or her disappearance throughout the community. On the National Center for Missing and Exploited Children (NCMEC) website, there are a number of cases that illustrate the effectiveness of issuing an Amber Alert. Within days (and in many cases, hours), children have been safely recovered from abductors who became aware that the child's disappearance was being broadcast. Since its inception in 1996, at least 495 children have been located alive as a result of this emergency response system. However, the majority of these recovered missing child cases using Amber Alerts involve noncustodial parents who have kidnapped their children.

Greenville police officials explained their reasons for not issuing an Amber Alert for the missing teen. The chief of police, Daniel Busken, explained that "early on, we had only limited time and only a certain amount of information to deal with. . . . Even until now, we aren't sure Alicia was abducted."[37] In conducting research on this case, I was taken aback at Officer Busken's assertion. First, one would think that the chief's acknowledgment of "limited time" would necessitate an immediate notification of Alicia's disappearance since in most cases with missing and endangered persons, victims are killed within hours of their abduction. Second, since Alicia was a minor and the family indicated to authorities that her absence for such a long period was not typical, an Amber Alert appeared to be in order to locate the missing girl. And third (and most pertinent), Alicia Moore's mother informed authorities that her daughter had been sexually assaulted only months before her disappearance, and the alleged perpetrator was in jail awaiting trial on rape charges in her case.[38] How the latter point was not sufficient to categorize Alicia as a missing *and* endangered person is astounding.

While her murder is at the time of this writing still under investigation, it is clear that a murdered witness cannot testify against a sexual assailant. If anyone had a motive in making certain that Alicia disappeared, it would certainly be her accused rapist (or perhaps someone working on his behalf). For this reason, it seems implausible to many why the revelation of her being a victim of sexual assault was not enough to warrant a statewide emergency response. In a later news article, police released a statement explaining that they believed Alicia to be a runaway, primarily because her mother divulged that she had "done this before but never stayed away this long" and had in the past befriended an older adult male.[39] However, Alicia's mother grew concerned about her daughter's absence after a *three-hour delay* in her returning from her bus stop and told police that her daughter had never stayed away "that long." One could question whether three scant hours would constitute runaway status.

As stated previously, the sexual integrity of black females is called into question in many missing person complaints, and in some cases, very young victims are still treated with suspicion. In Toni Irving's examination of 2,000 rape complaints that were ignored by Philadelphia police, one victim was only seven years old, and yet the case was labeled "investigation of the person." The police treated the young victim as a lost child, even though a man who knew her mother kidnapped her from the front of her babysitter's home and raped the child in a car at a nearby park. When the assailant kicked her out of the car and the child ran to safety, she was hysterical and told her babysitter what occurred. After the police were notified, they failed to take the child immediately to the hospital for an examination, and it was not until her mother rushed home from work and demanded the police examine her child for sexual assault that she was taken to the hospital for a rape kit examination. Blood and semen were found in the child's vaginal area as well as evidence of penetration. Nevertheless, the case remained dormant for four years until an exposé about misconduct in the department's handling of rape cases led the police to pursue and prosecute the perpetrator.[40]

In yet another case of a white missing Texas teen, police were aware that fourteen-year-old Haylie White *did* in fact run away with her thirty-three-year-old male neighbor with whom she was having a sexual relationship. Conversely, in this white missing person case, an Amber Alert was issued.[41] The girl's mother, Jan Nixon, became aware of an "inappropriate" relationship with Jacob Daniel West, a neighbor who also had lived in Haylie's home due to problems with his own family. According to media sources, Jan Nixon attempted to stop the relationship, but her daughter was insistent in maintaining her friendship with West. Furthermore, this was not the first time police had been notified about Haylie's taking off with her adult boyfriend. One week before she fled with West in front of her parents, the teen's grandmother called 911 because the girl had left home to be with him. She was recovered by the police, and she was returned home.

In a final act of desperation, Haylie's mother sent her daughter to live with other relatives to keep West from having contact with the girl.[42] Nevertheless, on January 22, 2013, while taking a walk with her mother and other family members, Haylie broke away from her family and jumped into Jacob West's SUV and fled with him. Jan Nixon stated to the press that she attempted to stop her daughter from leaving with West, even going so far as to hold on to her legs while she got into the truck.[43] Unlike with Alicia's disappearance, an Amber Alert was issued immediately upon Haylie's parents contacting the police, despite the fact that Haylie was indeed a runaway who repeatedly defied her parents' attempts to protect her from a sexual relationship with an adult predator. The alert was canceled on January 28, 2013, after the teen was safely located at a motel in Fort Pierce, Florida, and police acknowledged at that time that Haylie "didn't fit the criteria" for an Amber Alert.[44] It is interesting to observe how Haylie's case was framed in the media, also. Rather than describing the teenager as rebellious and wayward, she seemed to be characterized as a naive and pressured young girl who fell under the spell of a manipulative predator. Such may have been accurate; however, in Alicia's case, the press released an article explaining that Alicia's mother said she had been away from home before and had a past friendship with an older man. These details could be construed to paint a picture of the teen as precocious or culpable in her disappearance, thus making the public less sympathetic or concerned about her plight. Interestingly enough, a pattern of running away and being involved with an older man *was* true of Haylie White, yet efforts were exerted by law enforcement to locate her and return her safely to her family. Could race have played a part in this obvious incongruity?

To the media's credit, while they did not provide coverage regarding Alicia Moore's case when she was first reported missing (not surprising when the police categorized her as a runaway), the press featured a number of stories about her family's anger with law enforcement's failure to issue an emergency response to locate the teen. This helped galvanize the Greenville community to march in protest against the slow response of the police in investigating the murdered teen's disappearance.[45]

REAL HOUSEWIVES . . . REAL DIFFERENCE IN MEDIA
COVERAGE: THE CASE OF TARA LYNN GRANT (WHITE)
AND LIZZIE MAE COLLIER-SWEET (BLACK) (2007)

In 2007, in the state of Michigan, news outlets were overrun with stories of the homicide of a white female, thirty-four-year-old Tara Lynn Grant, whose husband of nine years, Stephen Grant, murdered and dismembered her, dumping parts of her corpse in a nearby wooded area. Her initial disappearance and subsequent murder became headline news around the country, as well as daily breaking news as each detail of the case emerged from police sources.

On Valentine's Day of that year, Stephen Grant phoned the police and informed them that his wife, Tara Lynn, had left their upper-middle-class Washington Township home several days prior after an argument about her increasing travel responsibilities as part of her employment. He claimed she got into a black sedan and was not seen again. Stephen Grant was a stay-at-home dad who provided daily child care to the couple's two children while his wife was a successful general manager at an engineering firm. According to media sources, Stephen Grant became irate when his wife informed him that she needed to travel to Puerto Rico on business after returning from the country only a day earlier. He later confessed that during the argument, he struck her and began to strangle her as she fought valiantly for her life. After killing Tara, he took her body to his family's machine shop, where he dismembered her and scattered parts of her corpse throughout a wooded area not far from the couple's home.[46] Police initially suspected Stephen Grant in Tara's disappearance and engaged in daily surveillance at the couple's home, while Stephen provided a number of interviews with the press, tearfully asking that his wife return home. After a woman walking through the wooded area found a bag with metal shavings and what appeared to be human blood and took this evidence to the police, a search warrant was issued to search the Grant home. Stephen Grant then fled in a borrowed neighbor's truck; police located him forty-eight hours later in a wooded area in Northern Michigan, where he was suffering from hypothermia and frostbite. A search of the residence uncovered the missing woman's torso. Police discovered other parts of Tara's body in the wooded area location where the bloody bag was found.

Concurrent with Tara Lynn Grant's disappearance and murder was a less well known missing woman named Lizzie Mae Collier-Sweet. Collier-Sweet has been missing since early January 2008, after her house was mysteriously set on fire.[47] Police officials had publicly stated that they believed Collier-Sweet had met foul play, and her estranged husband, Roger Sweet, has remained the primary suspect in this case. Shortly after his wife's disappearance, Brownstown Township police charged Roger Sweet with several counts of sexual assault against minors, possession of child pornography, and second-degree murder in the death of his first wife.[48] While there were parallels in the stories between Grant and Collier-Sweet—both were believed to be victims of homicide by an intimate partner, and both of their disappearances generated media coverage (in Collier-Sweet's case, however, to a lesser degree)—there is one major difference between Grant and Collier-Sweet. Lizzie Mae Collier-Sweet was black. She was one victim of color among many who are routinely ignored by the media and, in essence, are "invisible" as victims of violence.[49]

The media prominently featured stories about Tara Lynn Grant, and there was even an article in *People* magazine about her murder that was salaciously titled "Mr. Murderous Mom."[50] The Grant murder case dominated not only the local evening news headline stories in metropolitan Detroit but also received national coverage and garnered nineteen articles in the *Detroit Free Press* alone (I did not count the number of articles found in the *Detroit News*). Major local newspapers in Detroit (both the *Detroit Free Press* and *Detroit News*) provided daily coverage for more than thirty days, with most of the stories being featured on the front page and dominating the entire front section as well. Even among white victims, Tara Grant's case and the prominence and amount of coverage her murder received were exceptional. A looming question for many who were astounded by the volume of press this homicide received was, in essence, what was so extraordinary about this victim and her death while similar homicides of many African American women (and some white women) were virtually ignored by the media and/or generated substantially less attention?

It is important to note that Tara Grant was an educated and upper-middle-class woman who lived in one of the wealthier communities in Michigan. Her income alone supported her entire family, as her husband did not work and was their children's primary caregiver. Perhaps in the case of Tara Grant, one could argue that both race and social class impacted the newsworthiness of her death.

Discussion of the disparity in news coverage between the two cases occurred frequently among Michigan residents; even police officials were frustrated that the Tara Grant case overshadowed Collier-Sweet's disappearance, possibly impeding the latter case from remaining in the public eye and generating new tips. A reporter for the *Detroit Free Press*, Zlati Meyer, wrote an article on Collier-Sweet's disappearance and interviewed a detective in the case who expressed disappointment in the public's diminished interest in the story and the small reward offered in the case.[51] Another article mentioned police frustration again: "Police believe the national media attention given to Tara Grant . . . somewhat overshadowed national attention in the Brownstown [Collier-Sweet] case. . . . Police are counting on the media to help now so that another year won't go by with police, family, and friends having to ask the same question again." [52]

The disappearance of Lizzie Mae Collier-Sweet came to a tragic end when, on March 28, 2013, her body was discovered in a shallow grave less than a mile from her home. Collier-Sweet's body was buried with her clothing, and personal identification was found in the pocket of her jacket. When Channel 7 Action News in Detroit announced the discovery of her body, I was anxious to hear the news since her disappearance was one of the cases featured in both my dissertation and this book. However, I was disappointed that despite the fact that Collier-Sweet had been missing for close to six years, the discovery of her remains was not the first story featured that evening. Eight other stories preceded the mention of Collier-Sweet being found; the lead story that evening was about frozen food at local Michigan markets being contaminated with E coli bacteria, followed by a "Right to Work" legislation protest.

The seventh story was a feature about Pope Francis washing the feet of juvenile offenders on the eve of Easter Sunday weekend. Clearly the producers of the news program thought that even the discussion of a flood at a residential dormitory at the University of Michigan was more important than the announcement of a long missing and possibly murdered woman's body being recovered. Not only had excessive and prominent coverage about Tara Lynn Grant's murder eclipsed Lizzie Mae Collier-Sweet's disappearance, but the discussion of a small number of college students losing laptops to a flood in their dormitory ranked higher than the unearthing of her body in shallow grave.

INNOCENCE LOST: THE CASE OF CHANEL PETRO-NIXON (BLACK) AND IMMETTE ST. GUILLEN (WHITE AND VENEZUELAN) (2006)

On Father's Day, June 18, 2006, sixteen-year old Chanel Petro-Nixon told her parents that she was going to apply for a job at an Applebee's restaurant and left her home with a promise to return shortly. She was never seen alive again. Four days later, her body was found in a trash bag on the sidewalk in front of an apartment building only blocks away from her home. According to news sources, she was partially clothed and had been strangled; her cell phone and designer athletic shoes were missing. Her mother, Lucita Nixon, reported her daughter missing on Monday morning, allowing the necessary time before a missing person's report could be filed with the police. However, despite protestations from Chanel's parents that she was an honor student and had never run away from home in the past, the officer taking the complaint wrote "runaway" on the file. The word "runaway" was incongruent with Chanel's reputation as a nerdy, scholarly student according to a neighbor and classmate: "She was really quiet. I would see her in the library at school all the time."[53] There appears to be an observable pattern of police categorizing missing African American females as runaways, much to the frustration and helplessness of victims' families. It could be suggested that this assumption is primarily based on the age of the victim—especially when she is a teenaged female. But there also seems to be another factor at play—race. Society's historical pattern of chivalrous protectiveness toward white females is evident in the prompt response by the media and law enforcement in the disappearance and/or murders of members of this racial group compared with that of racial minorities.

A more expeditious response by the media and law enforcement to missing young women (whose families emphatically urge that their daughter would never disappear voluntarily) could possibly prevent their homicides. In tragic fashion (as was the case in the murder of Romona Moore), it was determined through an autopsy that Chanel was alive at least forty-eight hours before her death, again confirming the need for immediate intervention in her disappearance.[54] Had police acted quickly, it is possible (no matter how remote) that they could have saved her life.

Furthermore, hypervigilance by the media and law enforcement toward murder victims is also necessary to stir public sentiment and outrage leading to aggressive investigations to apprehend their killers. This pattern was epitomized in the brutal murder of Immette St. Guillen, a twenty-four-year-old Upper East Side resident of New York City and graduate student at John Jay College of Criminal Justice. On February 25, 2006, St. Guillen and her friend Claire Higgins went to a downtown Manhattan bar called Pioneer for a night of fun and drinks. The bright and attractive graduate student was only three weeks shy of completing her degree and wanted to unwind. However, several hours into the night, Higgins thought it was time to head home and urged her friend to leave with her by cab. Despite the fact that it was after 2:30 A.M., and both were already inebriated, St. Guillen wanted to go to another bar. Higgins refused, got into an argument with St. Guillen, and then left by cab. The image of Immette St. Guillen walking down the street to another bar haunted her friend during the trial of her accused killer. "I stood there and watched her walk away."[55]

According to news reports, St. Guillen wandered into another bar called The Falls, where she had several more drinks before closing time. Although the bar's owner, Daniel Dorrian, did not initially inform the police that he asked the bar's bouncer, Darryl Littlejohn, to escort St. Guillen out of the bar (she reportedly became irate after being refused more drinks as the bar was closing), he reluctantly admitted such was the case. "I didn't want to get involved," he testified in court.[56] Dorrian also testified that he last saw St. Guillen being put out of the bar through a side entrance by Littlejohn; her body was found the next day, wrapped in a blanket and dumped on the side of a road in Brooklyn. The assailant bound and gagged her, forcibly penetrated her vaginally and anally, beat and choked her, and then suffocated her with a sock in her throat and plastic tape around her head and face.[57]

The people of New York City reacted strongly and angrily to the young woman's killing. A barrage of news coverage (both print and televised) immediately followed the discovery of St. Guillen's body, with the *New York Times* producing more than forty-five articles on her murder and the *New York Post* covering the story with no less than eighty-five articles, most on the front page of the paper. Fox News covered the case as a top story within a week of the young woman's body being discovered. The onslaught of media and law enforcement attention on the case culminated in the arrest, trial, and conviction of The Falls' bouncer, Darryl Littleton, for the rape and murder of Immette St. Guillen in May 2009. St. Guillen's body was found on February 26, 2006; Littlejohn was arrested on March 6, 2006—approximately one week later.

The death of Immette St. Guillen also had significant legislative impacts. On August 16, 2007, the city council of New York City passed a law that required all clubs and bars operating within the city to hire only licensed bouncers. Additionally, club owners were required to "install cameras at all exits and entrances, purchase high-tech ID scanners to ferret out fake IDs and compel bars with underage drinking violations to hire NYPD-approved monitors."[58] In a final quest for justice for Immette, the St. Guillen family sued the federal government for $100 million in a wrongful death lawsuit, alleging that the convicted killer, Darryl Littlejohn, was insufficiently monitored while on probation at the time Immette was murdered. The family accepted a payment of $130,000 and the renaming of a computerized probation tracking system in Immette's honor.[59]

Conversely, both the families of Romona Moore and Chanel Petro-Nixon tried and failed to get legislative measures passed to prevent the tragedies that led to their daughters' deaths. Moore's mother called for a law titled "Romona's Law" that would require the immediate investigation by law enforcement of the disappearance of anyone under the age of twenty-five who has been reported missing by family members. According to Sean Gardiner, of the *Village Voice*, "Romona's Law was discussed at one hearing before the City Council's Public Safety Committee in December of 2004 and hasn't been brought up since."[60] Likewise, Chanel Petro-Nixon's family and supporters pushed for an "always search" policy that would require police officers to "seriously and fully" investigate a report of a missing person when the family of the victim believes the missing person is the victim of an abduction.[61] To date, this initiative has not been implemented by city of New York or the NYPD.

The perpetuation of invisibility and the devaluing of these unfortunate black female homicide victims were not only carried out by the media and law enforcement. Even the Greenville school district was negligent in issuing an alert to warn other students about Alicia Moore's disappearance. When confronted by a local News 8 reporter and asked about the lack of warning to parents on the school's website after Alicia went missing, Greenville Independent School District (ISD) superintendent Donald Jeffries responded, "No, but I mean . . . so what?"[62] Jeffries's response of "so what?" encompasses the entire focus of this book. His obvious indifference to Alicia's disappearance and murder is a reflection of the larger society's disregard for vulnerable victims of color.

CHAPTER 3

AN UNEASY ALLIANCE

The Symbiotic Relationship between

the Media and Law Enforcement

ON A NUMBER OF OCCASIONS, I REACHED OUT TO THE MEDIA TO interview journalists and editors to hear their side of the issue regarding racially biased coverage. I sought to ascertain what factors make a story newsworthy. Furthermore, I wanted to understand how editorial decisions are made with respect to which homicides are covered and whether the race of the victim plays a part in which stories receive more prominent coverage. My first attempt at contacting members of the media was through phone calls, followed by a standard email:

Hello X,

My name is Dr. Cheryl Neely and I am a professor in Sociology at Oakland Community College. I graduated from Wayne

State University in May of 2009 with my PhD in Sociology and I am currently writing a book based on my dissertation topic—media's coverage of African-American women as victims of homicide. This is an often talked about, but rarely written about topic in academia, and I am interested in getting members of media (actual reporters and instructors in the field) views on this issue. I have formulated 6 questions for a brief interview and I would very much like to interview you for my book. If you'd like to discuss this further (and I hope that you are), I can be reached at (office) or by (cell). I can interview you face-to-face over coffee (my treat) or over the phone . . . whichever is convenient for you. I look forward to your response to this request.

Sincerely,
Cheryl Neely, PhD

The questions I developed for the interview were designed to gauge the perspective of the journalist on accusations of biased reporting for female victims of homicide:

1. What in your opinion makes a story about homicide "newsworthy"?
2. Does race play a part in determining newsworthy coverage either directly or indirectly?
3. How do you as a journalist respond to criticism about media's apparent bias in covering stories related to minorities that are missing and/or murdered?
4. In your experience/opinion, which type of homicide victim receives prominent coverage?
5. What is your opinion regarding media's power in increasing police response in investigating/solving of homicides involving "prominent" victims (prominent victims are those receiving extensive, top news coverage)?

6. Does racial/ethnic diversity among reporting/editorial staff impact how stories are written about minority victims? Does it make a difference?

Unfortunately, despite a plethora of emails, phone calls, and even sending reporters previews of the questions I wanted to ask, it seemed that my efforts were rebuffed time and time again. In one case, I called the editor of a local newspaper on at least four different occasions, even speaking with his secretary, imploring her to let him know the nature of my call. Instead of returning my call, the editor told his secretary to advise me to speak with an associate editor, who then told me that the person I should be speaking with was the very editor I was attempting to interview! Nevertheless, the associate editor asked that I forward her the questions, which I did promptly; I never heard from her again. I began to suspect that the sensitive nature of this topic and trenchant criticism of the media regarding apparent racial bias in their coverage of stories contributed to their reluctance to go on record. I was unable to obtain direct answers to my inquiries, and thus I turned to literature and media studies research to answer my questions.

NEWSWORTHINESS AND VICTIM DISCOUNTING

In August 2011, Robin Barton, a legal journalist and former assistant district attorney, wrote an article entitled "Missing White Women Syndrome" and explicitly stated that race "is the biggest factor in determining how much interest journalists seem to show in a missing person's case."[1] She pointed out that when white females are missing, journalists act as though these cases are deserving of prominent news coverage, and she quotes Eugene Robinson, from the *Washington Post*, as describing white female victims as "damsels." Robinson suggests that the common denominator for these women, besides gender, is that "of course the damsels must be white."[2] It is disheartening to consider that a female who is a victim of violence is only viewed as vulnerable and deserving of rescue (hence the term "damsel") when she is white. The

41

terror, frustration, and faltering hope felt by the family members of Romona Moore, Chanel Petro-Nixon, Alicia Chanta Moore, and Michelle Jackson (among many others I did not mention) as they begged law enforcement and the media to find their "damsels in distress" was met with indifference and insensitivity. Perhaps it is because these victims were black and, as Robinson suggested, therefore did not meet the criteria of a female in peril.

It appeared that Barton, herself a journalist, was critical in her ability to extract honest answers from media colleagues about the role race plays in news coverage, and she cites several of her sources by name. Their candor was unexpected and refreshing. For example, Kevin Drum, of the *Washington Monthly*, revealed that ratings and advertisement dollars are tied to white female victims being more newsworthy because they get more viewers. Kristal Brent Zook, a Columbia University professor of journalism, argued that white females receiving more coverage is as much an issue of class as it is of race: "The virginal, pure, blond princess is missing. . . . It has a lot to do with class, sexuality, and ageism, not just race."[3] However, I would challenge Zook in her claim of class having a significant impact. In my research on this topic, I have encountered victims who were young, attractive, educated, and middle class who were also African American, yet the media attention was not there or was minimal at best. Class may indeed be a factor, but when other things are equal, race often trumps class in the United States. There is no shortage of research to support the discriminatory impact of race. Even in stories where white female victims were economically disadvantaged and, as such, were suspected of having a history of prostitution and/or drug use, there were attempts by reporters to provide a positive view of these victims despite their unsavory past. In my research, I recall more than a few stories that illustrated this pattern of reporting. In one case, the murdered and burned body of twenty-one-year-old Anke Furber (a white female) was found in a vineyard near Atlanta in 2006. According to the *Atlanta Journal-Constitution*, Furber had "been struggling with a drug problem" but was looking forward to being jailed for a bond violation to "get away from drugs."[4] Further, the reporter wrote: "Furber went to Sprayberry High School in Marietta, but began to get off course after she graduated. . . . [Her mother] remembers her daughter as a sweet girl who was a talented painter and who dreamed of being an artist."[5]

The article also included a number of interviews with family members and friends, and descriptions of Furber's cat, Suki, and her "stuffed animals, paintings and poetry." It was as though the writer sought to humanize the victim to offset a scornful public that would attribute the victim's death to her own culpability given her drug-addicted lifestyle. In yet another story about a white female victim, an article on the brutal murder and dismemberment of seventeen-year-old Jennifer Chambers in October 2007 begins, "By the time she was 17, Jennifer Chambers had already made a lifetime's worth of mistakes. Unlike most kids, she will never have the opportunity to undo them."[6] Despite her young age, Jennifer already had a history of crack cocaine abuse and prostitution, and the writer of the article describes her descent into self-destruction and a troubled history of foster care homes, drug use, and prostitution. The journalist states explicitly, "It was a sad, violent, end to a tumultuous life." Even the detective investigating her murder, Steve Rotella, took a sympathetic view of Chambers's death, declaring that "she didn't have a chance to correct her mistakes, and that's not fair. . . . Everything else is of no consequence to us." While I agree that the senseless murders of these two young women were shocking and abhorrent, and that their past salacious history should not have precluded public sympathy or a rigorous investigation into their deaths, I submit that stories about murdered women of color who were drug addicts and/or sex workers are also worthy of the same humanization and dogged law enforcement attention.

Unsurprisingly, a reporter's willingness to provide a compassionate view of the victim may be directly related to the race of the reporter, as I discovered in my own doctoral dissertation research. Robin Barton also confirmed the importance of diversity in newsrooms. She argued that when reporters are white, they are tempted to feel more empathy for victims similar to themselves, and having a racially and ethnically diverse reporting staff increases the likelihood that news coverage will more accurately reflect the larger community.

The broadcast news adage "if it bleeds, it leads" suggests that violent crime ranks high on the list of priority news. As such, violent crimes such as homicide are often reported as newsworthy based on both perpetrator and victim characteristics. Stories featuring women and children as murder victims have increased not only the number of viewers of evening news programs but also the sales of newspapers, as viewers and readers have visceral reactions to crimes committed against these groups.[7] Additionally, in many cases, the media may devote more time to crime stories based on characteristics of the victim that will provoke a greater level of public shock or disbelief. Homicides with female and child victims are seen as crimes that deviate from the norm and are thus considered important stories for newspapers to cover.[8] In other words, the greater the social status of the victim or the deviant nature of the crime, the more likely the story is considered newsworthy and gets attention from the media. Research indicates that homicides most likely to get coverage are deviant in terms of the infrequency of occurrence (a phenomenon known as statistical deviance), the high status of the victim, the shock or "perversion" of the crime, and whether the killing violates formal norms of a society.[9] Typically, murders of children or young females, particularly those committed by strangers, are reported as headline news, yet the brutal murders of victims such as Alicia Chanta Moore and Chanel Petro-Nixon, who were presumably the victims of stranger homicides, received little press coverage.

Moreover, since female victims of homicide are rare compared with male victims (statistical deviance), but have lower social status than men (referred to as low status deviance), these cases may not be considered newsworthy when one combines both types of deviance. However, I observed that when the female victim (low status deviance) is white (statistical deviance) and of a middle-class background (high status deviance), these factors in combination act as powerful predictors of newsworthiness by editors.

The act of determining which victims are salient enough for media attention essentially entrenches the belief that some victims have less value. Victim discounting (the act of not giving particular victims of violent crimes the same level of concern as other victims of violent crimes)[10] is perpetuated by the news media's omission or the underreporting of black homicide victims, particularly females. When one compares the actual number of homicides of black women with the proportion of coverage this group receives from the media (as I have done in this research), the conspicuous inequity begs explanation. Moreover, when black victims are contrasted with their white counterparts, the imperceptible status of black women is difficult to deny. Laci Peterson, Michelle Young, and Tara Grant were all white female victims of suspected intimate-related homicides, and each case received extensive nationwide coverage from major broadcast and print journalism outlets. Yet for every Laci, Michelle, and Tara, it is more probable that minority women will be murdered by intimate partners yet receive little media attention in comparison.[11]

Indisputably, when the media concentrate on particular issues, the public follows suit. The focus on blacks as criminals (particularly males) is very common. Evening news programs are replete with minorities over-represented as perpetrators of violent crime, but more rarely as victims.[12] In particular, crimes involving white victims and black assailants receive the most extensive coverage. In doing so, the media are reinforcing long-standing stereotypes of black males as criminals and capitalizing on whites' fears of victimization by minorities.[13] Despite repeated denials by the media that race is a determinant in decisions regarding newsworthy coverage, research on this issue refutes their assertions. Essentially, racial stereotypes perpetuated by repeated coverage of black males as criminals increase whites' concerns about crime as well as support for more severe punishment for these offenders.[14]

Additionally, politicians (especially conservatives) exploit these fears and suggestively make white fear of black crime a platform for election. George H. Bush's use of an African American murderer named Willie Horton during his 1988 presidential campaign against Michael Dukakis helped to catapult him into the White House as he ran on the platform of being tough on crime. Horton became a symbolic representation of the type of black male criminal whites feared most.

The sociologist Richard Lundman points out that not all murders make the news, and of those that do, only particular murders become major news stories. Since local news stations are under pressure to bring in high ratings (which in turn increases advertisement dollars), stories most likely to receive prominent coverage are those that reflect the concerns of white society.[15] This is not to suggest that most whites do not care about crimes that happen to victims of other races; however, people in general tend to identify with victims from similar social categories. Since whites are the dominant group in the United States, the media tend to placate this group in an effort to increase ratings and newspaper subscriptions. Both print and broadcast journalism are highly competitive in a race to provide breaking news coverage and garner a larger share of the market's subscribers and viewers.[16]

To facilitate quick reporting of current news, it has been found that journalists report stories based on typifications or stereotypes that reflect the existing social structure.[17] By doing so, not only do they provide stories that the general public can identify with, but they also reinforce inequalities and racial and gender hierarchies.[18] With such pressure to show blacks as criminal offenders, there tends to be less interest in showing them as victims of crime. Murders with white victims and black assailants are more likely to get newsworthy status and prominent coverage since they are rooted in white fear of blacks and white racism.[19] The "scripts" for these stories exist and have for centuries. Likewise, murders of women by men also confirm assumptions about male dominance and female vulnerability. However, not all murders of women by men make the news—slain women of color do not receive the level of media coverage that white females get, especially when the killer is most commonly a black male.

As several studies indicate, these crimes do not strike a chord of fear in the heart of white Americans (since the victims are racially different), and therefore might be dismissed as a common occurrence and/or reflective of a minority group's perceived cultural shortcomings. While searching Boston newspapers online for more information about a series of serial murders of black women that occurred in the city in the 1970s, I stumbled upon an article from the *New York Times* from the year 1971. The article, titled "Police Seek Clue to Stamford Murders," covered the killings of five black women in Connecticut; their bodies were dumped in an affluent, mostly white area of the city. The reporter wrote: "The killing [referring to the last victim found, Alma Henry] seemed to have evoked interest but little fear and no panic among the residents of the predominantly white city of 108,000." Several local residents were interviewed, and one man stated that if the killings had been similar to the Boston Strangler murders of the early

1960s, "everybody would have been scared . . . but don't you see it's not that type of killing."[20]

Most of Albert DeSalvo's (the accused killer in the Boston Strangler murders) victims were white females, with the exception of one black female, twenty-year-old Sophie Clark. The neighbor's use of the term "everybody" seems to imply that whites are representative of most people, and because the Stamford killings were of black women, victims who also had a history of prostitution and drug use, their deaths were insignificant. Another resident, a married woman with children, expressed her concern about the homicides, but fear was not the basis. "We don't like being made a dumping ground," she said. "I just hope the next body doesn't turn up on my stone fence or in the pool. It would scare the daylights out of my children."[21] Incredibly, this woman's worry was not about the fact that a possible serial killer had been murdering victims of her sex. These victims were neither of her race nor her class, and therefore she did not believe her personal safety was in jeopardy. She simply didn't want the bodies (like trash) dumped on her property where her children might find them; her attitude demonstrated a callous disregard for human beings who had been brutally murdered.

COLLABORATING FOR JUSTICE—THE MEDIA AND LAW ENFORCEMENT

The relationship between the media and law enforcement presents an interesting, yet ironic dichotomy. On the one hand, the media act as an ally to police by bringing crimes to the attention of the public in the hope that doing so will generate tips that will help solve the homicide. However, on the other hand, the media's relentless quest for "breaking news" can result in a premature or erroneous leak of information that compromises the crime investigation. Therefore, the two entities form an "uneasy alliance"—one needing the other to be effective while simultaneously viewing each other as a hindrance. However, when it comes to getting justice for a victim, the beneficial consequences of media attention in the clearance of homicide cases by police cannot be underestimated. This point was reinforced several times in interviews I conducted with members of law enforcement, which included homicide detectives. I interviewed four members of law enforcement, specifically officers who actively investigated homicides in the Detroit and Detroit metropolitan area. The questions I formulated for the interview were as follows:

1. To what extent do you believe media plays a role in which homicides are a top priority to investigate?
2. Have you ever felt pressured by media officials or members of a community to solve a violent crime? If so, please describe.
3. Have you ever been assigned to a violent crime case or taken off of a case by a commanding officer against your own personal objections? If so, do you believe personal characteristics of the victim played a role (class, race, sex, etc.)?
4. In your personal experience/opinion, to what extent does race and sex of victim play a part in homicide investigations?

When asked what role law enforcement thought the media played in murder investigations, Brandon Harris, an administrator with the Detroit Police Department, explained:

> I believe the media plays a significant role in homicide investigations and law enforcement investigations in general, but most specifically homicide investigations. Due to public pressure from certain communities such as the business community, [these are] the people who seem to get priority in certain investigations as far as media coverage and the desire to get some type of closure. I was just remembering there were cases in the past where certain high powered people within the city or the city government had some type of affiliation or connections with the media and were able to have a lot more pressure.

Lieutenant Robert Grant, of Brownstown Township Michigan, was the chief homicide investigator in the Lizzie Mae Collier-Sweet case. When I interviewed him in November 2013 regarding his view of the media and victims of homicide, he expressed a positive view of journalism, primarily at the local level:

> I'm a firm believer in media helping law enforcement rather than going after police officers. A lot of law enforcement officers have different opinions on the media. I've been doing this for 28 years and I've had nothing but good luck with the media and especially even in the Lizzie Mae Collier-Sweet case. The local media was just exemplary, they were fantastic . . . from channel 2, 4, 7 . . . they were fantastic through this whole thing.

According to Lieutenant Grant, the media's ability to get information to the public provides a very necessary resource when police are trying to gather information to solve a homicide. Even though some people would hold a disdainful view of reporters' aggressive tendency to press individuals for information, including family members of victims, Grant saw the value in this approach. In many cases, it provokes possible witnesses to notify the police with information that might be helpful in finding the perpetrator. He explained, "You know some people say, 'look at them sticking a mike in that poor family's face.' A potential witness might say I can't let this go on. . . . I need to do something even though I wasn't going to say something." He did, however, concede that not all members of law enforcement hold a favorable view of the media and may see their intrusion as an impediment in homicide investigations. Yet Grant believed it best to maintain collaborative and respectful relationships with members of the press: "I don't think that they [media] push to solve. . . . I think they push to want to know. And basically to do their job. . . . The media is like any job that anyone else has. And . . . they're going to push and I think the more you handle them delicately . . . give them a little bit of what you can, I think it goes a long way. Like I said . . . that's repaid in dividends in what the media can do for you."

While Sergeant Kenneth Gardner, a homicide investigator with the Detroit police department, concurred with the opinion of both Officer Harris and Lieutenant Robert Grant that the media have some beneficial consequences

in generating public interest and action for victims of homicides, he also suggested that the media's relationship with law enforcement can potentially
damage a murder case:

> I believe that media has a strong impact on the way that homicides are
> investigated. It is actually two-fold. What I mean by two-fold is that it
> can play a negative as well as positive role as far as the crime itself goes.
> Positively, they can put specific information out there and get a plea out
> to the public that will help people to know about the story and generally
> may stimulate someone's heart to get involved and to take action in their
> community. But they can also be very negative in that aspect, too. They
> could put information out there that works directly against the solving
> of the crime.

Gardner added that the media might at times intentionally leak information
to the public or make implications about the background of a victim that
could complicate the case, stating: "Sometimes they [media] might put a
particular person or theme out there that they know is detrimental to the case
or they might give out too many clues or they may show some uh . . . I'm
trying to think of a way to put it . . . a person of the community that people
don't readily accept."

The latter part of Sergeant Gardner's statement refers specifically to
the way the media "construct" an image of the victim. Again, notions of
undeserving victims (the victim did not deserve or provoke his or her
death) versus deserving victims (he or she shares some of the blame for
his or her victimization) are a consequence of the manner in which the
media cover the news.[22] I asked Sergeant Gardner to explain further what
he meant by the media putting "someone out there that the community
might not readily accept." Was he suggesting that the media at times
provide an impression of a victim that makes the victim less sympathetic
to the public? As Gardner explains: "Correct . . . correct . . . and because
of that negative connection, people are less likely to get involved in aid-
ing the police in apprehending the person responsible. In other words,
you know, in a negative form, it can be to the point where people will say

'that person deserved to get killed!' In my opinion as a homicide detective, I don't care what you were doing in life . . . you don't deserve to get your life taken. Drug dealer, or whether you killed people yourself . . . if it's an illegal killing, it's an illegal killing!"

The fact that members of law enforcement see the media's ability to make the public pay attention to victims and thus possibly move viewers to action in providing tips reinforces the point of why the press is so important. While trying to determine the whereabouts of Lizzie Mae Collier-Sweet, Lieutenant Grant described to me how he repeatedly reached out to the media at the national level to find the missing woman: "That was my heartburn about the investigation. I needed the national attention to make sure that she wasn't out there somewhere . . . because we were getting no help from the husband. And that's why I wanted to reach out. She had family in Florida . . . she had family in Atlanta. And I wanted that national media attention. And for whatever reason . . . I would simply say that it was because it was just a missing person in the city of Detroit area. I think if it would have been some other big city . . . I think it would have gandered [*sic*] more media attention. I have no idea . . . but nobody wanted to help. Nobody wanted to touch that."

Lieutenant Grant's frustration was palpable, but he stopped short of attributing the national media's (specifically *Dateline NBC*) reluctance to cover Lizzie Mae Collier-Sweet's disappearance to race (despite the fact that they provided extensive coverage of Tara Lynn Grant's homicide). As a homicide investigator for almost thirty years, Grant denied ever allowing race to hinder his commitment to getting justice for murder victims. In fact, after reading in the *Detroit Free Press* a comment he made about being frustrated that there was not enough attention from the media to Collier-Sweet's disappearance, I was very interested in interviewing him for this book. Nevertheless, when I asked him if he thought that race played a role in the lack of attention Collier-Sweet received as a missing person, he seemed to have difficulty believing that such was possible: "God . . . I'm sure there are people out there who will argue with me, but I would not even want to fathom or think that that would ever happen in this day and age and especially in law enforcement. I don't want to believe that . . . I have never seen it in the more than 20 years. . . . I don't know if it's out there. . . . I don't think that media would run that way. And I just . . . cannot . . . we are a terrible society if that even would perceive to be happening."

What I found interesting about Lieutenant Grant's comment was that close to the end of our interview, he again expressed his disappointment in *Dateline NBC*'s refusal to come to Michigan to cover Collier-Sweet's disappearance, but immediately provided coverage to a story about a nine-year-old girl who drove the family van from a liquor store because her father was too drunk to drive. Grant stated that he could not recall the exact reason why the news program said it would not cover Collier-Sweet's disappearance, but he believed the excuse was related to time constraints. He explained:

> There is something else I found interesting. I had called uh . . . *Dateline NBC* . . . this is interesting to me just to show you the way this happens. I had called *Dateline* to ask them to work me and do something [in regards to Lizzie Collier-Sweet] because it was a very important story. Detroit Metropolitan area . . . house burned up, lady missing, husband's arrested. . . . All of that . . . but they said they couldn't run the story because of . . . time. But remember a couple of years ago when a nine-year-old girl was driving the van for her dad? He was drunk so he let her drive . . . and boy . . . they came from New York and they set up there and they came in and they did a big story with us about a nine-year-old child driving a car, but they didn't have enough storyline or timeline to do a story about a . . .

I finished the statement by adding "a missing and possibly murdered woman." He agreed emphatically, "Yes!" While it is highly unusual for a preadolescent child to be forced to drive for her intoxicated father, it was not lost on me that the little girl in question was Caucasian. It is highly questionable, in my opinion, that *Dateline* found this story to be more worthy of national coverage than a woman who went missing and whose home was burned down on the day of her disappearance, and when the suspect was her estranged husband who was also being charged in the death of his first wife. While Lieutenant Grant found it to be incredulous that the race of the victim would be a determining factor in media coverage, I countered that based on empirical research, facts confirmed that race is not only a factor in deciding which victims get prominent coverage but also in law enforcement's attention to certain victims. Officer Harris made this point clear during our interview when I asked him if he believed race played a role in the way homicides are investigated by police. "Uh . . . unfortunately yes . . . I do believe that race has some type of role in or have [*sic*] something to do with how certain homicides are investigated. I won't say priority, but I will say a little bit more attention is given to possibly white women and then of course, following that would be white males, and then of course um . . . blacks and others would follow after those two, but I believe those, especially white women, would have a greater sense of urgency and some type of investigative desires." Harris's "pecking order" or racial hierarchy of victims was echoed by Officer Frank Gregory, who agreed, "I would say, probably Caucasians would have just the higher priority . . . particularly white females."

A point I have made several times in this book is that reporting staff that encompasses racial and ethnic diversity is critical to ensure that news reflects a larger, diverse community, not just whites. It appears that the same is true for law enforcement, as Sergeant Gardner pointed out that he has observed white officers being less vigilant with minority victims compared to their response when victims of crime are white. The following is part of an exchange during my interview with him:

ME: To what extent do you feel the race or sex of the victim play[s] a part in homicide investigations? Do you believe that race has a role in priority investigations . . . or even if sex does?

GARDNER: Unfortunately . . . *yes* . . . I have experienced that . . . it's harder for certain races to get involved to the degree that they should be involved in their cases when it's not a person of their race. Uh . . . in my experience they have a tendency to not adequately investigate the case. Now . . . why do I feel that is part of race? Because I have seen people of their race or of another race (I guess you could say) be murdered and every resource that they can pull together is used to investigate that case . . . more time . . . more people are dedicated. So yes, race plays a part.

ME: Now to be specific, are you seeing this more with white or black victims?

GARDNER: I see this with um . . . white victims. And let me clarify . . . I can only speak for Detroit. That I see that when a white victim . . . not all the time . . . but I have seen where a white individual has been murdered and everybody is jumping to resolve it more quicker than if you had found an African American that had been killed in that same circumstance. Those same resources have not been dedicated.

Lieutenant Grant's personal and deeply felt commitment to solving violent crimes irrespective of the race of the victim appeared to be the primary reason why he could not imagine that certain victims would be ignored by the media, yet alone by homicide investigators. However, Sergeant Gardner's observation further confirmed a pattern of indifference that was apparent in the murders of many of the victims in my research, including that of my friend Michelle Jackson.

CONCLUSION

It is certain that media attention is a critical resource for law enforcement when it comes to solving homicides—especially murders committed by a stranger to the victim. News coverage acts as a conduit to provide awareness of a killing to the public. The media's ability to convey stories in an empathetic manner arouses the passion of individuals who might then channel their outrage into action. Even Grant made this clear in his interview when he discussed his efforts to contact national media outlets for help in solving the disappearance of Lizzie Mae Collier-Sweet. Further, Romona Moore's family beseeched media in New York to broadcast her disappearance but to no avail, and tragically, her death came after several days in captivity.

Since victims of color rarely get the level of media coverage that white female victims do, it can be tremendously advantageous to know someone who can influence the media. This was evident in the murder of thirty-two-year-old Rosaline Ransom-Lee in May 2013 in Pontiac, Michigan. The African American mother of three was abducted, raped, and then strangled by Bobby Lee Taylor, forty-two, a sex offender who was a stranger to the victim. Rosaline's sister Richelle is a close friend of Star Jones, a former prosecuting attorney and former cohost of *The View* and a contributor on *The Today Show*. Jones was able to reach out to her media colleagues through a series of emails (according to news reports, 180 were sent), asking them to broadcast the story of Ransom-Lee's murder, and the homicide was featured on Nancy Grace's program.[23]

When the national media covered the story, tips rolled in to the Oakland County sheriff's office, and within weeks, Oakland County detectives and the FBI interrogated Taylor. The police subsequently arrested and arraigned Taylor in the rape-homicide. According to the *Oakland Press*, Star Jones used her influence as a celebrity because she believed the murder of Ransom-Lee "could've otherwise fallen by the wayside."[24] Furthermore, she disseminated an email statement to the press about the case and argued that murders by strangers are more difficult to solve, "but this time, most of the cards were on our side."[25] Had Ransom-Lee's sister not be acquainted with an influential celebrity, would this case—the murder of a working-class, black single mother—have gained national exposure? I believe it is highly improbable that such would have been the case. Neither does Star Jones, who expressed her frustration about the lack of media attention to black female victims in a live interview with the Huffington Post. She stated that she thought it necessary to "scream from the rooftop" for the media to pay attention to murdered African American women if that is what it takes get the level of attention needed to solve the case.[26] Jones has also appeared on Nancy Grace's show discussing her observation of biased media coverage that favors white female victims over murdered women of color. Jones used Ransom-Lee's murder as a platform to make black women aware that in the event of their being victimized, they need to be prepared for the aftermath. She stressed that as common victims of violence and, in many cases, the primary caregiver for their children, it is urgent that they prepare themselves and loved ones for the possibility of an unforeseen tragedy or violent death and plan accordingly. Jones collaborated with several colleagues to create a list called "Rhonda's Rules," which was named after Rosaline Ransom-Lee (also known as Rhonda to her family and friends), who left behind three small children, including a ten-month-old daughter. Star Jones thought it important that women (especially single mothers) engage in estate planning and create a detailed inventory of their desires regarding personal belongings, financial affairs, and custody matters in reference to their children.[27] Jones continues to speak out on behalf of African American victims and is a strong advocate for the media to exercise balanced coverage for all victims, regardless of race.

I cannot stress enough that the purpose of the book, again, is not to devalue the lives of white female victims to advance attention to women of color. It is simply to demonstrate that all women, regardless of race, should be afforded the indispensable "capital" of the media when they fall victim to lethal violence. When the media work in collaboration with members of law enforcement, victims and their families have a better chance of obtaining justice against the perpetrators of their untimely deaths.

CHAPTER 4

LOOKING AT MEDIA BIAS IN
THREE MAJOR CITY NEWSPAPERS

Results of Author's Research

IN 2007, I BEGAN MY DISSERTATION RESEARCH ON THE TOPIC OF THE media's tacit discounting of African American female victims of homicide and decided to use newspapers to gather my data. Despite declining readership of newspapers throughout the United States,[1] I argued that newspapers remain a primary method for the general public to be informed on issues considered relevant and important for most of society. One common approach to collecting research information is to gather qualitative and quantitative data.[2]

A researcher can collect qualitative data using what is called a content analysis approach. In conducting a content analysis study, the researcher identifies the problem to study and conceptualizes the research questions. Additionally, he or she classifies the primary unit(s) of analysis (in my case, it was newspaper articles), develops a coding scheme, and, preferably, employs at least two people to code the data to ensure reliability.[3] For my research, I decided to use a content analysis of three newspapers—the *Atlanta Journal-Constitution*, the *Detroit Free Press*, and the *Washington Post*—examining articles written about single-victim homicides of females between 2005 and 2007 who were fourteen years of age and older. I selected single-victim homicides as opposed to victims who were murdered in a multiple-victim homicide since it is more sensational when more than one person dies violently at a crime scene. I selected articles where the female victim was fourteen years or older for the same reason. Inherently, younger victim and multiple-victim cases would garner more media attention.

I conducted the content analysis of the articles in two phases: part of my gathering of information from the articles included identifying and counting the number of story framing characteristics or indicators.[4] Story framing indicators are factors within the news article that contribute to shaping the reader's perception of the homicide and victim. Another term for this phenomenon is "media effects."[5] In essence, the media report news in a manner that influences the audience's understanding of the event and provokes emotional responses of fear, rage, sympathy, and so forth. Most newspaper stories on homicides include basic information such as the victim's name (if the victim was identified), age, some details related to the manner in which the victim was killed (depending on whether it was determined and/or whether authorities released this information to the public), and comments about the case from police officials investigating the crime. Beyond these basics, newspapers may include additional information about the victim's background, life experiences, employment at the time of death, level of education, interviews or comments from individuals who knew the victim and described the victim's personality or popularity, and so forth. As stated previously, the literature indicates that positive characteristics about the victim impacts the public's perception of the homicide and the response to it. I developed a coding scheme to record these characteristics for comparison and statistical evaluation across race as evidence of racial bias in reporting.[6]

Another feature of news stories that humanizes the victim is the inclusion of photographs of the victim. Photos are an important part of a story since the public tends to be "influenced by them considerably," primarily because a photograph makes the victim's death seem more personal.[7] In essence, when victims are portrayed in the press as individuals who made a difference or who mattered to others, the public is more likely to perceive that person as undeserving of her or his violent death. Such empathy might result in a very vocal demand that the perpetrator be punished. When victims matter to the press and are depicted as such, they matter to the public.

The decision to focus my research primarily on black and white female victims was borne out of difficulty in accessing homicide data on other racial groups. When I began the early brainstorming/planning stage of my dissertation topic, the initial intent of the analysis was to compare three different racial groups of homicide victims—whites, blacks, and Latinas. However, the number of stories with Latina homicide victims in the newspapers I selected was miniscule compared to African American women and would have been technically difficult to do, thereby skewing the analysis. Furthermore, the FBI's Uniform Crime Reports (UCR) only specifically identify white and black victims in their expanded homicide data tables, which report homicide victims by racial categories and record all other racial groups simply as "other races." Thus, it was considerably difficult to obtain national data on homicides by particular racial groups outside of white and black victims.

The FBI's act of collapsing the racial identities into just two categories was not an accident. During the late nineteenth century, the UCR began excluding other racial categories with the exception of whites and blacks, and this is rooted in the United States' history of tracking black criminality. Foreign-born immigrants were gradually eliminated from crime reports, and blacks became representative of the criminal class and were contrasted with whites, who represented the country's ideal of normalcy.[8] Likewise, victim categories were also constructed into two specific groups—whites and blacks, with all remaining races lumped together under "other." Given these data-mining challenges, I decided to track the victims by the two available racial categories.

Detroit has two major newspapers that cover crime stories in the Detroit metropolitan area—the *Detroit Free Press* and the *Detroit News*. I selected the *Free Press* for two reasons: the extent of its readership, and the extent to which the paper is known for its liberal bent in covering stories in metropolitan Detroit.[9] I assumed that a more liberal publication would provide more balanced coverage.

RESEARCH FINDINGS

Overall, the results of my research indicated that the media demonstrated a favorable bias toward white victims in their newspaper coverage of female homicides. There were obvious and significant differences in the actual number of homicides reported in the 2005 FBI UCR compared with the extent of newspaper coverage in regards to white females in two of the three Metropolitan Statistical Areas (MSAs)—namely Detroit and Washington, D.C.

- Less than 2 percent of homicide victims in the Detroit metropolitan area were white females, but 77 percent of the articles about female homicide victims were about white female victims.
- 7.2 percent of homicide victims in the Detroit metropolitan area were black females, yet only 23 percent of the articles about female homicide victims were about black female victims.

This would indicate that overwhelmingly, *almost all murders* of white females were reported in the *Detroit Free Press* newspaper while only a portion of homicides of black females were reported in the paper. In short, even though black females made up the majority of female homicides that year, only a fraction of those murders were covered by the newspaper.

Likewise, this same pattern was found in the *Washington Post* as well.

- 3.4 percent of homicide victims in the Washington, D.C., area were white females, but 55 percent of the articles about female homicide victims were about white female victims.

- 7.0 percent of homicide victims in the Washington, D.C., area were black females, yet only 45 percent of the articles about female homicide victims were about black female victims.

There was also a noticeable difference in the number of homicide stories between black and white victims as well; on average, there were 46 percent more articles written about white victims compared to black victims, and these differences were also present when I focused on city-level data (meaning that the data reflected only the city and not the surrounding suburbs) in Atlanta and Detroit. Furthermore, my analysis revealed the following across all three cities and their surrounding suburbs:

- 30 percent of the articles about white female homicide victims mentioned the woman's education.
- 19 percent of the articles about black female homicide victims mentioned the woman's education.

Again, photographs of the victim are powerful story framers for readers. In my analysis of the articles from all three newspapers, I found that there was a greater number of photos in news articles for white victims compared to black. Overall, there were approximately 87 percent more photos in white victim stories in comparison to those stories about black females.

This difference was even greater in the Atlanta newspaper—the total number of articles on white female victims in the *Atlanta Journal-Constitution* had on average 220 percent more photos compared to articles featuring black victims.

As I have stated before, the location within the newspaper where an article is placed reflects the importance or prominence of the victim. Typically, articles found on the front page or within the front or first section of the newspaper are more visible and more likely to be read than those stories buried in subsequent sections of the paper.

- 53 percent of the time, editors placed articles about white female homicide victims in the "other" section compared to 78 percent of the time for black female homicide victims.

- 49 percent of the time, editors placed articles about white female homicide victims on the front page, front section, or front of other section.
- 25 percent of the time did editors place articles about black female homicide victims on the front page, front section, or front of other section.

Finally, findings from the *Washington Post* articles also showed bias toward white victims in the location of the story: I located articles on the murders of white victims to a greater extent in the more prominent sections of the newspaper.[10] One case in particular stands out as receiving less prominence than it deserved. On January 23, 2005, the body of a twenty-four-year-old black woman named Sherine Williams was found on the bathroom floor of her apartment near Washington, D.C., by family members. After trying in vain to reach her by phone, and having the police refuse to forcefully enter Williams's apartment, Sherine's brother and sister broke into the apartment through a window and discovered their sister's bloody body (she had been pistol whipped, shot, and slashed in the throat) on the bathroom floor.[11] This horribly brutal homicide of a (by all accounts) shy and good-natured data clerk appeared in the *Washington Post* in the "B" section of the newspaper.

Although there were subsequent articles written about the homicide, they primarily focused on her killer, twenty-nine-year-old Daunteril Hall, and his efforts to avoid the death penalty. The victim and the accused killer did not know each other, which made this case a stranger homicide—the type of murder that tends to get the most attention from the press. Nevertheless, the mention of the victim in the few articles that were written seemed to serve primarily as a reminder of Hall's crime. As it was in the case of my friend Michelle's murder, Sherine Williams was not the focus of these news stories, and the location of the initial article on her slaying demonstrated that her murder did not rate "front page" news.

It is important to note that my analysis across all three city newspapers revealed that editors placed articles about white victims more often on the front page or in the front section of the newspaper than they did stories about black victims. In other words, the difference in location of white and black victims' stories was not due to chance, but was statistically significant; it reflected a systematic and deliberate pattern of racial bias that was consistent in each of the newspapers, with the exception of the *Detroit Free Press*, which, having so few articles about black victims, made the bias of that particular paper not statistically significant. Historically, in times past, African Americans were forced to sit in the back of the bus. How ironic it is that now as victims of homicide, their stories are found in the back of the newspaper.

Another measure of the status of the victim is the word count or length of the article. In short, how many words were used to inform the public of the victim's homicide? Longer articles provide an opportunity to include more details about the victim and of the murder; there is usually more background information about the victim and comments from grieving and traumatized family members, friends, and neighbors. I found that across all three newspapers:

 Articles pertaining to white victims were longer and had a larger word count compared to those about black victims.

- In the *Atlanta Journal-Constitution*, the difference in word count between articles on black and white victims was 258 words versus 508 words, respectively.
- The inequity in article length was more pronounced, however, in the *Atlanta Journal-Constitution*.

Again, these patterns appeared to be systematic and deliberate. Moreover, I wanted to investigate whether the reporting bias in favor of white victims in the findings was a function of reporter bias or coincidental. Not surprisingly, I found that the race and gender of the reporter factored in the word count, with reporters showing bias toward same-race victims. In other words, white reporters wrote longer articles on white victims, and black reporters (although a small percentage of reporters writing the articles used in my analysis) wrote longer articles about black victims. Given that such was the case, articles about black victims may have been shorter since black females constituted only 4 percent of the reporters who authored the articles. Additionally, white female reporters were not only biased toward white females in writing longer articles, but they were also more likely to mention the victim's education level, describe the victim in a positive manner, and use emotionally laden terms to describe the homicide (for example, "brutal," "gruesome," "tragic," and so forth).

One striking way the media demonstrate how a victim is valued is by the comments featured in the story that were made by influential members of a community. In particular, I found that some of the articles tended to include positive comments about the victim's personality and statements from high-ranking officials, such as a city administrator or a police chief. In one case in Savannah, Georgia, there was extensive media coverage of a white female who was robbed and shot to death by a black assailant. Several high-profile politicians in Georgia expressed their outrage about the crime to the media and stressed their commitment to get justice for the victim and her family. David Simons, a Republican political consultant, boldly exclaimed, "Crime in Savannah now has a face, and it is the face of a 19-year old girl who is the daughter to many of us!"[12] Never mind the fact that violent crime had routinely plagued African Americans living in the poorer neighborhoods in Savannah—when a random act of violence happened to the daughter of an elite white family, it was time to get angry. It is hardly surprising that the story also appeared on the front page of the newspaper.

In an effort to test whether some of the story framing indicators and word counts could be used to predict the race of the victim, I used a number of statistical methods that revealed that word count, marital status, and the location of the article within the newspaper accurately predicted the race of white victims in my research. The story framing characteristic that had the most impact on predicting the race of the victim was marital status. In other words, if the marital status of the victim was mentioned in an article, the victim was most likely to be white.

Furthermore, it was more likely that a married victim's story would be located in a more prominent section of the newspaper to be noticed by the reader. Is it possible that the bias was not racially based, but reflective of a victim's marital status? To answer this question, I controlled for marital status and examined married victims across race and word count. The findings indicated that even when black victims were married, there was still bias toward white female victims: white female victims had, on average, 85 percent more words written about their deaths than black female victims. Thus, marital status did not elevate black victims to newsworthy coverage.

Even when black females were married, they had shorter articles that were buried in less significant sections of the newspaper. Tara Lynn Grant and Jane Bashara were both married women whose deaths received nationwide coverage in a number of media outlets (both television and print media). Lizzie Mae Collier-Sweet was also a married victim, but her murder received less media attention, even to the frustration of homicide detectives investigating her death. Each of the three women was married and was believed to have been murdered by her husband. However, Grant and Bashara were white, while Collier-Sweet was African American. It is hard to deny that the difference in coverage each victim received is reflected in her race.

DIFFERENCES BETWEEN CITIES

When I conducted individual analysis of the data by city, I found that there was greater disparity in reporting homicides of black and white victims in Atlanta compared to Detroit and Washington, D.C., particularly when it came to the location of the story in the newspaper. Homicides of white female victims were featured in more prominent sections of the Atlanta newspaper, specifically on the front page or in the front section of the paper. In fact, of the three newspapers, the *Atlanta Journal-Constitution* had the longest articles on white female victims. While there was statistical bias favoring white female victims across all three MSAs, Atlanta accounted for most of the significance.

The explanation for this phenomenon may lie in the historical and political backdrop of the city of Atlanta. Often touted as "a city too busy to hate" during the civil rights era, African Americans enjoyed a standard of living that was not attainable by most blacks living in the South. Forging a place for the "black elite," Atlanta became a hub for black progressives and intellectuals, as whites began to move out of the city to outlying suburbs. The historian Kevin M. Kruse has argued that the white exodus from Atlanta (like the white flight in Detroit after the 1967 riots) resulted in the preservation of segregation (in the form of all-white suburban communities and counties) as the United States was ending Jim Crow policies in response to the civil rights movement.[13] It would stand to reason that the obvious racial disparity found in *Atlanta Journal-Constitution* articles is essentially a reflection of the institutionalization of racism in the social structure of the city, despite political and economic progress made by African Americans in this urban metropolis. Despite the progress African Americans have made since the civil rights movement, Atlanta, and the state of Georgia as a whole, still maintains patterns of discrimination against blacks in its criminal justice system, health care institutions, employment, and even the public transportation system. [14]

Moreover, the current underlying racial tension in Atlanta that has been a source of contention between blacks and whites in the city stems from young African Americans flocking to Buckhead, a prominent and mostly white community in Atlanta, for entertainment and the club scene, much to the consternation of white residents.[15] Whites pressured lawmakers to pass an ordinance to close clubs two hours earlier and advocated for more police presence near these establishments, which resulted in the harassment of black youth and allegations of police brutality. Thus, it appears that despite the progress blacks have made living in this region (many of its current citizens are new transplants from the North), elements of racism are still embedded in the infrastructure and attitudes of whites in Georgia.

It appears that of all three newspapers, the *Washington Post* had more balanced coverage and less racial bias in its reporting of homicides. While there was only one black female reporter who wrote the articles selected for this study, the reporter wrote shorter articles for black victims than for white victims. This was the only time that a reporter of a particular race demonstrated no bias in article length in stories of victims of his or her racial group. In both the *Detroit Free Press* and *Atlanta Journal-Constitution,* when the reporter was an African American female, the average word count for black victims was greater than that for white. One possible explanation for the more balanced coverage of black and white female homicides in the *Washington Post* seems to lie in two factors: the diversity of its reporting staff, and the overall racial demographics in Washington, D.C. (see tables 2 and 3).

Based on a review of table 2, one can see that

- In the *Washington Post*, there was more ethnic diversity in the category of "other" reporters than in the *Detroit Free Press* or *Atlanta Journal-Constitution*.
- In the *Washington Post*, 24 percent of the reporters were of Asian, Latino, and Indian descent.
- The *Atlanta Journal-Constitution* had only four "other" reporters (all of Latino descent).
- The *Detroit Free Press* had only two reporters in the "other" category (one of Latino descent and one of Asian descent).

This data suggests that an important consequence of greater racial diversity among the reporting staff is that the race of the victim is less of a factor when an article about a homicide is written. When journalists of varying racial backgrounds make up the staff of a newspaper, it appears that when they report on stories about homicide victims, racial bias is significantly diminished.

Table 2. Race of Reporter by City Newspaper

Reporter Race/Gender	Atlanta Journal-Constitution		Detroit Free Press		Washington Post	
	N (36)	%	N (39)	%	N (50)	%
Black Female	4	11	1	3	1	2
Black Male	6	17	2	5	9	18
White Female	5	14	14	35	12	24
White Male	17	47	20	51	16	32
Other Female	2	6	1	3	6	12
Other Male	2	6	1	3	6	12

Moreover, as can be observed from table 3, the residents of Washington, D.C., have a higher education level and median household income ($61,835) than people living in Detroit or Atlanta. However, blacks appear to fare better in Detroit when it comes to the number of African American–owned firms (64 percent) compared to almost 31 percent in Atlanta and 28 percent in D.C. It is worth noting that both Washington, D.C., and Atlanta have a comparable black/white population ratio and bachelor degree and higher attainment ratio, yet bias toward white female victim homicides was more prevalent in the *Atlanta Journal-Constitution* than in the *Post*.

CONCLUSION

Previous research in the area of media bias in race and crime highlights the overrepresentation of black men as assailants and white females as victims. Again, this pattern reinforces the invisibility of black women as the more common victim of violence, particularly at the hands of black males. The

Table 3. Demographics of Atlanta, Detroit, and Washington, D.C.

Atlanta	*Race*	*Median Household Income*	*Bachelor Degree and Higher*	*Black-Owned Firms*
Black	54.0%	$45,946	46.1%	30.9%
White	38.4%			
Detroit	*Race*	*Median Household Income*	*Bachelor Degree and Higher*	*Black-Owned Firms*
Black	82.7%	$27,862	12.2%	64.2%
White	10.6%			
Washington, D.C.	*Race*	*Median Household income*	*Bachelor Degree and Higher*	*Black-Owned Firms*
Black	50.7%	$61,835	50.5%	28.2%
White	38.5%			

Note: Data extracted from U.S. Census Bureau State and County Quick Facts, 2011 estimates.

analysis provided in my research for the most part confirms the media's neglect of black women as victims and the need for social action to address the antecedents of this violence. It also calls for an investment in solutions to eradicate it, and increased media attention is a viable first step.

Perhaps one of the most important findings my research unearthed is that greater racial diversity among newspaper reporters and editors may have a diminishing effect on discriminatory or racially biased reporting. This was powerfully illustrated in my data from the *Washington Post*.

CHAPTER 5

MAKING THE INVISIBLE VISIBLE

Minorities' Efforts to Obtain
Recognition for Forgotten Victims

MOSTLY FROM AN ANECDOTAL PERSPECTIVE, MANY AFRICAN AMERI-
cans have observed that both the media and law enforcement have been slow
in responding to crimes committed against black victims. Even as I researched
cases of homicides of black female victims in newspapers, particularly for the
case studies presented in chapter 2, I noticed that victims' families frequently
complained that their murdered loved ones were not receiving the same
attention given to white victims and their families. Unfortunately, despite
these emotionally charged conversations around water coolers and kitchen
tables, there is a lack of academically published research to substantiate the
extent of this phenomenon. I was both surprised and disappointed when I
conducted a literature review to develop the theoretical basis for my doctoral dissertation, and found the information to be woefully inadequate in
addressing the disparity in media coverage for black female homicide victims.

Ironically, this reinforced assertions that black women, as victims, are both invisible and devalued despite their violent and brutal deaths.

Within the black community, the frustration concerning this phenomenon continues to grow. The impatience is evident in the plethora of blogs, social media sites, recent television programming, and community activism that have emerged to demand media attention toward African American wives, mothers, and daughters who fall victim to foul play, yet fail to garner the reaction and resources needed to solve crimes against them. Thus, some members of the black community have turned to the Internet and other means to make the invisible visible.

A number of social scientists and critical theorists have referred to the use of social media as a catalyst for political action as "Internet activism."[1] Since the 1990s, groups have organized and engaged in dissemination of information, protests, and resistance campaigns around impassioned social issues. The expediency and efficiency of social media in spreading information throughout society (that is increasingly dependent on technology) have become a frequent topic of research in the academic literature.[2] To that end, African American activists have embraced the use of social media as a means of resistance in creating a forum not only to vent about the lack of media attention and widespread apathy by white society toward homicide victims of color but also to chronicle these victims' violent demise in an ongoing macabre tally. The black community is no longer waiting for the mainstream media to broadcast stories about the murders of black women. They have pursued the outlets of social media and Internet blogs to voice their outrage and push for justice for the victims. This chapter explores the use of these Internet resources and community outreach to increase awareness and outrage that moves the public from apathy to social action and justice for murdered black women.

JOURNAL DE LA REYNA

Described as a "very informative blog" in August 2007, Journal de la Reyna, an anonymous Internet site, featured an overview of the media's discounting of black victims through three cases of the serial murders of black women: the Boston Murders (1978–1979), the Southside Slayer Murders (1980s and 1990s), and the Henry Louis Wallace Jr. serial killer case (1992–1994).[3] I came across this site accidentally while gathering data on female homicides, and Journal de la Reyna became a primary reference source for me to examine cases of community activism by African Americans. This blog was established to increase more news coverage and amplify responsiveness by law enforcement in black victim homicide investigations. Before encountering this website, I had never heard of the aforementioned cases of serial killings, which was surprising given my more than thirty-year proclivity in following homicides in newspapers. Paradoxically, the fact that someone like myself, a person with an extensive interest in violent crimes committed against women, had not heard of these horrific cases of serial murders was surprising. I suppose this is the purpose of such a blog—to inform the general public about cases of homicide with forgotten black victims.

The first case the unnamed author of the blog described was a series of twelve brutal sexual murders of black women (suspected by the black community to be the work of a serial killer) in Boston during 1978 and 1979. The Boston police countered that the killings were committed by several killers and not linked, further enraging residents of the community. The women were killed within a two-mile area encompassing the predominantly African American communities of Roxbury and Dorchester. There were very few articles available from news sources regarding these murders. Most of the information came from the Combahee River Collective, a black feminist group in Boston that led a protest in 1979 against the Boston police for their slow response to the homicides.[4]

Not only had the African American community been outraged that the homicides received little to no press in the *Boston Globe*, they also complained that law enforcement seemed lackadaisical in their failure to aggressively investigate the killings. Also troubling was the fact that the police refused to acknowledge a link in the homicides suggesting the work of a lone serial killer, and categorized each of the victims (eleven African American women and one white woman) as prostitutes.[5]

73

There were a number of protests, led mostly by black and white feminists who were part of the Coalition for Women's Safety, to demand more action from law enforcement to apprehend the individual(s) responsible for the murders.[6] In one such incident, more than 1,500 members of the community marched to protest the callous disregard for the twelve victims, and according to the website, community leaders were relentlessly accused by the *Globe* of race-baiting a city already fraught with racial tension and hostility. In response to the *Globe's* indifference, the city's black news publication—the *Bay State Banner*—ran front-page coverage daily about the homicides and the community's increasing anger toward the mainstream media and the Boston police.[7]

The website Journal De La Reyna, despite not having an identifiable blogger, was an excellent source in providing information about grassroots efforts by the African American community to draw attention to neglected victims of homicide, specifically black women. For example, the blog also posted an article written by Christine Pelisek, a *LA Weekly* reporter who had covered a series of murders of black women that occurred in Los Angeles over a twenty-five-year period, much to the chagrin of members of the Los Angeles Police Department (LAPD), who feared the coverage would "tip the killer's hand." The killings, which began in the mid-1980s, were initially referred to by the press as the Southside Slayer murders, but eventually were called the Grim Sleeper murders. The slayings of ten black female victims continued for a number of years, then appeared to suddenly stop, and then to start again thirteen years later; hence the name the "Grim Sleeper." Pelisek was commended for providing media attention to a string of brutal murders of black women, most with histories of drug abuse and prostitution. The victims had received little press coverage, and the homicide investigation into their deaths was considered less than satisfactory by the south Los Angeles black community. One of the primary criticisms of law enforcement's response was that despite the fact that the string of murders had similar characteristics, the homicides were not readily considered the work of a single killer. Furthermore, families of the victims were not notified that there were other murders of women that fit the pattern of their murdered loved ones. Pelisek noted:

So many "body dumps" were occurring that angry South Central and South L.A. residents lashed out at police, and in 1986, two years before Margette (the sole survivor of the killer) was raped, shot and left for dead, community members launched the Black Coalition Fighting Back Serial Murders. The coalition bitterly complained that "the low-profile media coverage and problems with the investigation are all examples of women's lives not counting and black prostitute women counting least of all."[8]

The Black Coalition Fighting Back Serial Murder, an organization founded by community and women's rights activist Margaret Prescod, was very vocal in its criticism of the LAPD, and relentlessly pressured police to investigate the Grim Sleeper homicides. Coupled with their anger at law enforcement, members of the group (primarily consisting of the victims' family members) were equally critical of the mainstream media for the lack of coverage of the killings (with the exception of Pelisek's exposé on the case). Prescod's primary concern was the fact that police were not forthcoming with information to the public that the killings were possibly the result of a serial killer, and thus women were not sufficiently warned to be more vigilant and careful in their daily routines. In an interview with CNN radio in 2009, Prescod excoriated the media for not valuing the lives of the victims, particularly since these women had histories of substance abuse and prostitution. Furthermore, she expressed the community's outrage toward the LAPD for not alerting the public (particularly black women) that a serial killer was on the loose, and no woman was safe until the culprit was apprehended:

> We knew . . . and everybody knew very well that if 11 women had been killed in Beverly Hills, or even in North Hollywood, you know there would be a national outcry, much less the little what was going on with these particular set of murders. These groups of people, no matter what you think of what they do in the line of work or whatever reason that they do it, it's almost like their lives don't matter . . . or don't matter as much as someone else. And that is one of the things that we were really outraged by. Because you know one of the things we said was is

that every time a woman leaves her house at night, whether it was to go and buy milk or go to work, she was at risk! And the police knew she was at risk and didn't tell her. That's playing Russian Roulette with women's lives.[9]

The mobilization and social action of the coalition finally paid off when, in 2010, a suspect was arrested in the Grim Sleeper murders—nearly twenty-eight years after the first homicide. Lonnie Franklin Jr., a sanitation worker in Los Angeles, was charged with ten homicides and, at the time of this writing, is waiting to go to trial. Police found Polaroid photos of the victims and of a number of other unidentified women that seemed to be taken shortly before the women were killed.[10] One victim survived an attack by Franklin; she was shot in the chest, raped, and pushed out of the vehicle. She lived to describe Franklin to the detectives and identify him in a police lineup.[11] Even though a suspect has been arrested and charged with the crimes, families of the victims are still frustrated with the slow pace of Franklin being tried for the murders, believing again that their loved ones have little priority in the court's administration of justice.[12]

Despite a record number of serial murder cases with African American female victims occurring throughout the United States over the past forty years, these homicides rarely received national media attention, primarily because many of the victims have past histories involving substance abuse and/or the sex trade. These victims have little to no value for many in society who view them as individuals who precipitated the violence committed against themselves. However, even when the victims are young and attractive women without salacious personal backgrounds but have respectable employment histories, their homicides still failed to meet the criteria for newsworthy coverage.

For example, in 2013 Journal De La Reyna featured a series of murders of young black women in Charlotte, North Carolina, committed by Henry Louis Wallace Jr., who was convicted in 1997 in the rape and murder of eleven women from 1992 to 1994. He is presently awaiting execution in a North Carolina prison at the time of this writing. Many of the victims knew him as a friend of the family or worked under his supervision at a Taco Bell restaurant. Because they knew and trusted him, the victims let him into their homes, where he viciously sexually assaulted and strangled them.[13] Wallace killed eleven young women before police finally became suspicious that his familiarity with the victims and their families was a common thread in each of the homicides. According to the few news sources written on the case, Wallace even attended the funerals of the women he murdered and volunteered to be part of search parties to locate several of the victims' bodies.[14]

As was the case in many serial murders of black women, it was difficult to get information from newspaper sources to confirm information found in online summaries of the Wallace case. A search of older newspapers yielded few articles; however, one article posted in the *New York Times* in March 1994 encapsulated the criticism leveled at the Charlotte police department for failing to aggressively investigate the homicides of Wallace's eleven victims.[15] The title of the article, "2 Years, 10 Murders, One Question," went right to the core of the controversy—how did one man carry out one of the worst killing sprees in North Carolina's history without detection and apprehension by law enforcement? Many of the city's African American community leaders, including those in the NAACP, believed that the race of the victims played a major role in detectives' dereliction of duty in solving these murders. Dee Sumpter, the mother of Shawna Denise Hawk, a twenty-year-old who was found raped, strangled, and face up in her bathtub, was very vocal in her criticism of the police department: "All of the victims were African-American women. . . . When you look at the races of all of the individuals, you can only draw the conclusion that race played a part in how the investigation was handled. . . . They deserved more attention that the Charlotte police gave them."[16]

Dee Sumpter and Judy Williams, the godmother of Shawna, together formed the social action group Mothers of Murdered Offspring (MOM-O) in 1993 to constructively channel their outrage at homicide investigators. They relentlessly pressured the police to forcefully investigate the murders and to bring the killer to justice. As a result of MOM-O's dedication, Henry Louis Wallace Jr. was arrested in 1994. MOM-O now has a website and

Facebook page where it routinely informs the public about the homicides of African American youth and broadcasts rallies aimed at reducing violence in Charlotte's black community.

Sadly, a pattern I found repeated with apparent serial murders of black women was the lack of articles that would have initially informed the public that African American women were being murdered, since it seemed that a number of bodies piled up before the first article about the homicides was even published in the paper. As Margaret Prescod noted in her criticism of the LAPD, women who are unaware of a serial predator are at risk for victimization when they are not informed that they must be more vigilant about personal safety in their communities.

"WHAT ABOUT OUR DAUGHTERS"

I began reading about homicides in newspapers when I was seven years old. As morbid as that sounds, it became a lifelong predilection, especially when violent crimes were committed against children and women. The unsolved Oakland County Child Murders of the 1970s created an atmosphere of anxiety and terror for children and their parents all over Michigan, and I read about the homicides and police investigation into the murders daily. I could even recall the names of the victims from memory and details from the crimes that most people did not want to discuss, let alone think about. But it was not some gruesome curiosity that led me to read about murders of other human beings. It was fear—fear that that particular victim could have been me. Perhaps I even thought that the more I knew about homicides, the better I would be able to protect myself from becoming a victim. Ironically, I pursued the field of sociology, and one of my areas of interest was violence against women. Both my master's thesis and doctoral dissertation focused on female homicides. But even after more than forty years of reading and studying details of murders, there are stories about lethal violence that literally take my breath away and sicken me to my very core. Thanks to Gina McCauley's blog, "What About Our Daughters" (WAOD), I became aware of a case that had that very effect.

In October 2006, the bodies of Quiana Jenkins-Pietrzak and her marine sergeant husband, Jan Pawel Pietrzak, were discovered in their San Diego, California, home. Both had been beaten, tortured, and shot execution-style in the back of the head. Quiana, who was African American, had been sexually assaulted with a vibrator while her husband, who was white, was forced to watch after being bound and gagged.[17] The couple had only been married two months before their murders. Tragically, Quiana was in the process of completing thank-you cards at the time the murderers forced their way into the newlyweds' home.[18] The perpetrators of the vicious murders were four marines who once were under the command of Sergeant Jan Pawel Pietrzak. They claimed the motive for the murders was robbery, but family members of the couple believed otherwise. Racial epithets and insults were written on the walls of the victims' home, and it was alleged that two of the killers, Emory John and Tyrone Miller, maintained a long-standing vendetta against Pietrzak when they worked under him at Camp Pendleton.[19]

In a blog titled "Why? Quiana Jenkins-Pietrzak Week—Day #1 Identifying Morally Indifferent Reporters," McCauley featured the story of the Pietrzak murders on the website to draw attention to what the blogger believed to be a lack of coverage of the brutal slayings and the trial of their killers. She wrote:

> In 2008, four marines raped, tortured and killed Quiana Jenkins-Pietrzak and her husband Sgt. Jan Pietrzak. That alone should have made her crime noteworthy. But in addition to the brutal manner in which she died, her husband was the commanding officer of her killers. We're merely asking why news outlets have decided to ignore this story for five years. Please use this form to identify reporters and outlets who have covered same or similar stories. On Wednesday we'll publish the list.[20]

The blogger spearheaded a campaign to galvanize readers to challenge the media to explain why the Pietrzak murders did not meet the criteria of newsworthy coverage and provided an online form to generate a list of specific reporters and news outlets that readers believed should have covered the story. McCauley even published a form letter to assist readers in contacting the media in case they had some concerns about how to compose an inquiry about news coverage of the case:

> I read your article about XYZ. Are you aware of the trial of four Camp Pendleton Marines who murdered their superior officer, Sgt. Jan Pietrzak, along with torturing and killing his wife, Quiana Jenkins-Pietrzak, execution style? The case has been ongoing for five years. This case seems as significant as the one you wrote on XYZ. Can you explain the decision-making process that went into covering XYZ while not covering the brutal murder of an officer by his subordinates and the rape, torture and killing of his wife on U.S. soil?
>
> Thank you for your participation.

A number of readers responded to the request and provided an update, with several stating that they sent emails to Nancy Grace and the Dr. Drew television show demanding to know why the Pietrzak case was not featured on their programs.[21] They also went a step further to point out that both Grace and Dr. Drew followed other homicides on their shows that were far less gruesome than Quiana and Jan's torture-slayings. One reader forwarded a copy of a response from Brian Moss, head of Ethics and Standards for Thomson Reuters, a multinational media and information corporation. The letter addressed the reader's concerns about the lack of coverage of the Pietrzak murder case and suggested that uncertainty in the outcome of a trial was the determining factor in whether it would receive prominent coverage. Moss argued that it was highly unlikely that the couple's murderers would be found not guilty, and thus there was no intrigue that would hook viewers. The letter read:

> Hi,
>
> Your comments were forwarded to me. I appreciate your interest in the decision-making process regarding our trial news

coverage. News coverage involves many choices. Many critics complain that too many news stories are insignificant. Editors reply that readers want to be entertained as well as informed. Some choices are determined by geography. Reuters, as a large international news organization, will make different decisions than a local U.S. newspaper.

Because two trials are happening at the same time doesn't mean that both would be of equal interest to readers—at least in the eyes of editors, who decide what stories Reuters covers. While there are many factors to consider—what sort of crime, what were the crime's details—a big part of what makes a trial of interest to readers is whether there is doubt about the outcome. Consider the O. J. Simpson trial. The murders of Sgt. Pietrzak and his wife five years ago are tragic, but the outcome of the trial of their killers was not unexpected. On the other hand, the controversy over the Trayvon Martin case has indicated there is wide interest in what will take place in the courtroom, and there appears to be no consensus on how the trial will end.

Sometimes editors make mistakes, and sometimes worthy stories go uncovered. Even the best staffed news organizations do not have enough people to cover as many stories as they'd like.

It is obvious that many people disagree with many of the choices that news organizations make. They certainly have the ability to seek out the coverage they're interested in at the many alternative news sources online. Thank you for taking the time to write, and thank you for visiting Reuters.com.

Sincerely,
Brian Moss
Ethics and Standards
Thomson Reuters

I am not certain that the tentative outcome of a trial is the primary reason why viewers tune in, as Moss suggested. I believe that the shocking nature of the crime and the trial's presentation of gruesome and explicit details of a murder are also factors that impact ratings, especially when the public believes the victims deserve justice. Consider the Petit murders in Cheshire, Connecticut, in July 2007. The home invasion and murders of Dr. William Petit's wife, Jennifer, and two daughters, Hayley, seventeen, and Michaela, eleven, by two men who were arrested leaving the residence after setting fire to the victims' bodies made the likelihood of conviction absolute, yet the trial was covered in great detail in both newspapers and television broadcasts. HBO even produced a documentary about the crime.[22] Furthermore, in concluding the letter, Moss's snide dismissal in seriously acknowledging the reader's concerns can be noted when he suggests that people can seek other news sources if they are not satisfied with Reuter's media. In short, if you don't like that way we cover the news, go elsewhere.

Activism through blogging is not new to Gina McCauley, the creator of WAOD. Named by *Essence* magazine in 2007 as one of the twenty-five most influential African Americans, McCauley has championed the cause of eradicating negative stereotypes of black women and demanding media attention for black female victims of violent crimes through her blog and self-published Kindle book, *More Than Words: How One Carb-o-holic Couch Potato Became a Cybercrusading Warrior Princess*. In August 2013, I conducted an interview with McCauley to discuss why she created the WAOD blog and what she hoped to achieve in her efforts to protect black women through engagement of social media.[23] The first question I asked her was what inspired the creation of "What About Our Daughters." She explained that the primary catalyst was a racist comment made by Don Imus, a conservative radio host, who referred to Rutgers University's black female basketball players as "nappy headed hos":

> You can read about it more in my book, *More Than Words*, but if you go back to the post of April 18, 2007, you will see that I started the blog in response to an Oprah Winfrey show in the aftermath of Don Imus

calling a group of college-educated Black women "nappy headed hos." Al Sharpton and the other black men on the panel were so dismissive of the concerns and feelings of a group of Spelman students who were participating in the show. I thought Black women had enough economic and political power to not have to put up with nonsense. Back then my theme was "Stop Funding Foolishness." It dealt with the idea of Black women punishing mainstream corporate America for funding Hip Hop's war on Black women. I thought I'd only write for a few weeks until I could find a group already working on this issue and then I'd write them a check and be done.

The blogger went on to explain that the principal goal of WAOD is "about Black women and girls and their issues coming first. Their lives aren't valued. Making sure they are not treated as collateral damage in the never ending race war. . . . We target sexism and misogyny in the black community in particular." Like Margaret Prescod, she stressed that media attention on victims of violent crime is invaluable in ensuring the safety of other potential victims as well: "Well, clearly more media attention means that the likelihood of recovering a victim safely or finding the perpetrators increases. Also, in the cases of serial rapists and killers, attention raises awareness so other women can attempt to take extra precautions."

While I described the actions of McCauley's collective inquiry of the media regarding the lack of media attention on the Jan Pawel Pietrzak and Quiana Jenkins-Pietrzak murders as activism, she maintained a different view. Her perspective was far more pragmatic and straightforward. She explained: "I didn't consider that activism. I just considered that asking a question. Sometimes you have to plant a seed and wait to watch it grow. It was important to let decision-makers know that we're watching what they are doing. I was actually shocked to see the response from Reuters."

It became clear to me through my interview with Gina McCauley that her frustration with the media's lack of regard for black female victims fueled her decision to create a forum to disseminate information and spark a conversation with readers to eradicate this indifference. Yet acquiring a large following of readers is not her priority. As she points out, the blog has been successful in achieving her goal of bringing attention to issues that are unique to black women, and almost eight years after starting WAOD, "I write because it is my primal scream to the Universe."

FIND OUR MISSING TELEVISION PROGRAM

The opening page on the website for the television crime program *Find Our Missing*, on channel TV ONE, features a silhouette photo of a young African American girl and asks the question, "Missing and Black: Where is the outrage?" The program, now in its second season, highlights missing person cases of African Americans and airs on a predominantly black broadcast station, TV ONE. Each week the show presents a case of a missing and believed to be endangered person of color and solicits tips from the public for information that would lead to the person's whereabouts. Viewers can even go online to theorize what they believed happened to the person and/or provide tips anonymously to assist law enforcement officials in their investigation. The fact that the show asks about societal outrage strikes at the heart of this book's premise in that it further confirms that public outrage acts as a catalyst for tips from the public and for law enforcement resources to solve the murder cases. The program is hosted by Emmy and Golden Globe award-winning actress S. Epatha Merkerson, who presents an impassioned and thorough overview of the case. Accompanying the story is a dramatization of the facts, which compels the viewer to stay tuned.

When I began viewing the program in 2011, the majority of the missing person cases featured were unknown to me, and I was surprised that a number of the victims had been missing for more than five years. With the creation of a program such as *Find Our Missing*, the public is provided information about missing persons that would not otherwise be covered in television and print news sources. Again, African Americans have constructed a vehicle to alert the public about victims of color who are missing and/or murdered, when they think that mainstream media has failed them to that end. A person who loses his or her life in a brutal act of violence should not remain in obscurity, particularly when the assailant has not been apprehended or held accountable for the slaying. With programs and blogs that express the African American community's "primal scream to the Universe" (as Gina McCauley so eloquently articulated), increasingly the invisible comes visible.

CONCLUSION

As a black woman, let me say that I am not a ghost. I exist as all other living creatures do, yet I do not always see an accurate reflection of *who I believe I am* in popular culture and the media. When images of black females manifest, they do so in the form of stereotypes and caricatures—from the angry black woman to the single mother of multiple children dependent upon welfare. It is hardly surprising that black women fail to foster sympathy from the larger society when they fall victim to tragedy, and as many cases in this book demonstrated, they are often seen as being culpable in their victimization.

In a world where concepts of beauty are predicated upon the physical makeup of women, historically racist ideology demeans African American women's distinct ethnic beauty, which has been virtually nonexistent in mainstream women's magazines. For centuries, black women's lips have been ridiculed as being too large, and their hips and derrieres were scourged as being abnormal and indicative of a primitive body type; yet today, some of the fasting growing cosmetic procedures are buttock implants, butt lifts, and injections. Despite the fact that black skin experiences a slower aging process due to melanin, few beauty magazines tout it as having inherent anti-aging properties. Even the magazine *Psychology Today* published a racist and highly contested pseudoscientific study by Satoshi Kanazawa, a professor at the London School of Economics who claimed that black women were less attractive compared to females of other races. He even suggested that African American women were less physically attractive than black men! Kanazawa based his findings on illogical, deliberately misinterpreted "data" and evolutionary measures of facial symmetry.[1] There was a swift and angry outcry against the magazine, and the editor quickly offered an apology. However, the article managed to contribute to the reinforcement of white society's discounting of black women's physical beauty. Perhaps the dismissal of black women as desirable females in a racially prejudiced public contributes to their marginalized, invisible status in a white-dominated society. From slavery through contemporary times, African American women were not protected from violence or recognized as legitimate victims when violated.

Typically when murders occur and receive media attention, the victim is thrust from obscurity to a tragic limelight. Moreover, the public's reaction in the form of outrage oftentimes leads to pressure on law enforcement officials and the criminal justice system to solve these killings expeditiously and bring the perpetrator(s) to justice. In short, in many cases the victim's *life* is valued, and the victim's *death* unearths the underlying fear that his or her unfortunate demise could have been the fate of any other innocent person, particularly when the perpetrator is a stranger to the victim.[2] However, as my research has shown, not all victims of homicide receive equitable attention from media news sources, particularly women of color. This conspicuous omission by the media in providing coverage of their violent deaths continues to be heavily criticized in recent years not only by the general public but by journalists and other members of the press as well.[3] Thomas Hargrove, a reporter for the Scripps Howard News Service, compiled a very comprehensive database of murders in the United States and found that in cases of homicide when the victim was black or nonwhite Hispanic, the clearance rate was 67 percent compared with 78 percent when the victim was non-Hispanic white.[4] Given that in many cases police vigilantly investigate murders of white victims and the media provide prominent coverage of the same, this disparity is not surprising.

Overall, black women's lives and experiences remain largely ignored by the general society, and at a time when they should be visible as victims of homicide, they still remain invisible compared to their white counterparts. Despite the fact that black women are at a disproportionately greater risk for being murdered, their deaths are not "front page news" nor are they part of the "breaking news" that dominates broadcast journalism outlets on a regular basis. The murders of white female victims such as Tara Lynn Grant, Natalie Holloway, Michelle Young, and Lacy Peterson will not easily be forgotten given that the circumstances of their deaths and/or disappearances have been ingrained in the consciousness of the American public through relentless coverage by the mainstream media.

However, for the numerous black women who were murdered during the same time frame and for the most part went unnoticed, there is no such comparison. It begs the question as to whether the media are responsible for the invisibility of black female victims of homicide or if the media simply reflect the disparity, the institutionalized racism, and the apathy inherent in the social structure of American society toward African Americans. It is my hope that this book has presented evidence of what is often assumed, but not necessarily confirmed, in a purview of the limited academic research and literature on this topic—that there is inequity in the treatment of murdered black females compared to murdered white females. The media must work actively to ensure coverage for all victims of homicides—regardless of race, sex, class, or any other factors that are the basis for discrimination. As articulated by the homicide detectives and other members of law enforcement I interviewed, justice for victims and their families depends on it.

NOTES

INTRODUCTION

1. Amanda K. Sesko and Monica Biernat, "Prototypes of Race and Gender: The Invisibility of Black Women," *Journal of Experimental Social Psychology* 46, no. 2 (2010): 356–60; Patricia Hill Collins, *Fighting Words: Black Women and the Search for Justice*, vol. 7 (Minneapolis: University of Minnesota Press, 1998); Signithia Fordham, "Those Loud Black Girls": (Black) Women, Silence, and Gender 'Passing' in the Academy, *Anthropology & Education Quarterly* 24, no. 1 (1993): 3–32; Patricia Hill Collins, "The Social Construction of Invisibility: Black Women's Poverty in Social Problems Discourse," *Perspectives on Social Problems* 1 (1989): 77–93.
2. Alice Walker, *In Search of Our Mothers' Gardens: Womanist Prose* (San Diego, Calif.: Harcourt Brace Jovanovich, 1983).
3. Kimberle Crenshaw, "Mapping the Margins: Intersectionality, Identity Politics, and Violence against Women of Color," *Stanford Law Review* 43, no. 6 (1991): 1241–99; William A. Darity Jr. and Patrick L. Mason, "Evidence on Discrimination in Employment: Codes of Color, Codes of Gender," *Journal of Economic Perspectives* 12, no. 2 (1998): 63–90; Lynne M. Vieraitis, Sarah Bitto, and Tomislav V. Kovandzic, "The Impact of Women's Status and Gender Inequality on Female Homicide Victimization Rates: Evidence from U.S. Counties," *Feminist Criminology* 2, no. 1 (2007): 57–73.

4. Ula Y. Taylor, "Making Waves: The Theory and Practice of Black Feminism," *Black Scholar* 28, no. 2 (1998): 18–28.

5. Kimberly Springer, "Third Wave Black Feminism?" *Signs* 27, no. 4 (2002): 1059–82.

6. Patricia Hill Collins, "Learning from the Outsider Within: The Sociological Significance of Black Feminist Thought," *Social Problems* (1986): 14–32.

7. Patricia Hill Collins, "The Tie That Binds: Race, Gender and US Violence," *Ethnic and Racial Studies* 21, no. 5 (1998): 917–38.

8. Ibid.

9. Ibid., 926.

10. Wayne A. Kerstetter, "Gateway to Justice: Police and Prosecutorial Response to Sexual Assaults against Women," *Journal of Criminal Law and Criminology (1973-)* 81, no. 2 (1990): 267–313.

11. Dorothy J. Imrich, Charles Mullin, and Daniel Linz, "Measuring the Extent of Prejudicial Pretrial Publicity in Major American Newspapers: A Content Analysis," *Journal of Communication* 45, no. 3 (1995): 94–118.

12. A number of studies indicate that the media significantly shape the general public's fear of crime as well as how sympathetic individuals are toward victims of crime. Among these studies are: John G. Boulahanis and Martha J. Heltsley, "Perceived Fears: The Reporting Patterns of Juvenile Homicide in Chicago Newspapers," *Criminal Justice Policy Review* 15, no. 2 (2004): 132–60; Jana Bufkin and Sarah Escholz, "Images of Sex and Rape: A Content Analysis of Film," *Violence Against Women* 6, no. 13 (2000): 1317–44; Brendan Maguire and Diane Sandage, "Crime Stories as Television News: A Content Analysis of National, Big City, and Small Town Newscasts," *Journal of Criminal Justice and Popular Culture* 7, no. 1 (1999): 1–14.

13. Travis L. Dixon, Christina L. Azocar, and Michael Casas, "The Portrayal of Race and Crime on Television Network News," *Journal of Broadcasting & Electronic Media* 47, no. 4 (2003): 498–523; Dixon, Azocar, and Casas determined that when blacks appear in news stories about crime, they are more often portrayed as perpetrators of crime and far less as victims. Whites are more likely to be featured as victims of violent crimes, and largely white audiences identify with the victim as a result this biased coverage.

14. Mira Sotirovic, "Effects of Media Use on Audience Framing and Support for Welfare," *Mass Communication & Society* 3, nos. 2–3 (2000): 269–96.

15. Daniel Romer, Kathleen H. Jamieson, and Nicole J. De Coteau, "The Treatment of Persons of Color in Local Television News: Ethnic Blame Discourse or Realistic Group Conflict?" *Communication Research* 25, no. 3 (1998): 286–305. Romer and his colleagues conducted a fourteen-week study of television news and noted a bias in the overrepresentation of minority groups (outgroups) as perpetrators of crime, while conversely, whites were portrayed more often as victims. As a result, ethnic groups were more likely to be blamed as perpetrators of violent crime, thereby increasing white outrage at crimes committed by minority groups and a demand for criminal prosecution.

16. R. M. Entman, "Modern Racism and the Images of Blacks in Local Television News," *Critical Studies in Mass Communication* 7 (1990): 332–45; Romer, Jamieson, and De Coteau, "Treatment of Persons of Color in Local Television News," 286–305; Travis L. Dixon, and Daniel Linz, "Race and the Misrepresentation of Victimization on Local Television News," *Communication Research* 27, no. 5 (2000): 547–73; R. M. Entman, "Television News, Prejudicial Pretrial Publicity, and the Depiction of Race," *Journal of Broadcasting & Electronic Media* 46, no. 1 (2002): 112–36; Travis Dixon and Keith Maddox, "Skin Tone, Crime News, and Social Reality Judgments: Priming the Stereotype of the Dark and Dangerous Black Criminal," *Journal of Applied Social Psychology* 35 (2005): 1555–70.

PROLOGUE

1. "Anti-Rape Program Praised," *New York Times*, March 25, 1984, A20.

2. "School Girl, 16, Found Slain in Garage," *Detroit Free Press*, January 26, 1984.

3. Ibid.

4. David Zeman, "How Justice Failed Eddie Joe Lloyd—Lawyers and Judge Did Little for Innocent Man Jailed for 17 Years," *Detroit Free Press*, October 24, 2002, A1.

CHAPTER 1. BLACK WOMEN AS HOMICIDE VICTIMS: REALITY VS. MEDIA REPRESENTATION

1. Marie Tessier, "Intimate Violence Remains a Big Killer of Women," womensenews.org.

2. "Lifetime Probability of Becoming a Victim of Homicide," in *Crime in the United States, Federal Bureau of Investigation* (Washington, D.C.: U.S. Department of Justice, 2000).

3. Ted Chiricos, Sarah Eschholz, and Marc Gertz, "Crime, News and Fear of Crime: Toward an Identification of Audience Effects," *Social Problems* 44, no. 3 (1997): 342–45.

4. Federal Bureau of Investigation, *Crime in the United States, 2011*, http://www.fbi.gov/about-us/cjis/ucr/crime-in-the-u.s/2011/crime-in-the-u.s.-2011.

5. Chicago's police superintendent, Garry McCarthy, confirmed to the press and public that in Chicago, particularly the areas of the Englewood and South Side communities, there had been an alarming 500 murders in 2012.

6. Sarah Stillman, "The Missing White Girl Syndrome: Disappeared Women and Media Activism," *Gender & Development* 15, no. 3 (2007): 491–502.

7. Anderson Cooper 360° Blog, Wikipedia, Encyclopedia Dramatica, and Free Thought Weekly Blog are among numerous Internet blogs that discuss biased media coverage of missing white females.

8. A number of studies have examined the lack of vigilance on the part of law enforcement in investigating violent sexual crimes against minority women. These include S. Lamb, *The Trouble with Blame: Victims, Perpetrators, and Responsibility* (Cambridge, Mass.: *Harvard University Press,* 1996); Janice Du Mont, "The Role of 'Real Rape' and 'Real Victim' Stereotypes in the Police Reporting Practices of Sexually Assaulted Women," Violence against Women 9, no. 4 (2003): 466; Jan Jordan, "Beyond Belief? Police, Rape and Women's Credibility," *Criminal Justice* 4, no. 1 (2004): 29–59; Phyllis A. Anastasio and Diana M. Costa, "Twice Hurt: How Newspaper Coverage May Reduce Empathy and Engender Blame for Female Victims of Crime," *Sex Roles* 51 (2004): 9–10.

9. "Bodies of 2 Missing Hamtramck Women Found Buried in Shallow Grave in Detroit," *Detroit Free Press*, March 25, 2012.

10. Ibid.

11. Richard J. Lundman, "The Newsworthiness and Selection Bias in News about Murder: Comparative and Relative Effects of Novelty and Race and Gender Typifications on Newspaper Coverage of Homicides," *Sociological Forum* 18, no. 3 (2003): 357–86; Richard J. Lundman, Olivia M. Douglass, and Jason Hanson, "News About Murder in the African-American Newspapers: Effects of Relative Frequency and Race and Gender Typifications," *Sociological Quarterly* 45, no. 2 (2004): 249–72; Darlene Rude, "Reasonable Men and Provocative Women: An Analysis of Gendered Domestic Violence in Zambia," *Journal of South African Studies* 25, no. 1 (1999): 7–27; Edith Greene, Heather Koehring, and Melinda Quiat, "Victim Impact Evidence in Capital Cases: Does the Victim's Character Matter?" *Journal of Applied Social Psychology* 28, no. 2 (1998): 145–56.

12. C. F. Bullock and J. Cubert, "Coverage of Domestic Violence Fatalities by Newspapers in Washington State," *Journal of Interpersonal Violence* 17, no. 5 (2002): 475–99.

13. Bill Laitner, "Man Kills Girlfriend, Then Self during Police Chase in Detroit." *Detroit Free Press*, July 6, 2012.

14. L. K. Gillespie, T. N. Richards, E. M. Givens, and M. D. Smith, "Framing Deadly Domestic Violence: Why the Media's Spin Matters in Newspaper Coverage of Femicide," *Violence against Women* (2013): 222–45; R. Taylor, "Slain and Slandered: A Content Analysis of the Portrayal of Femicide in Crime News," *Homicide Studies* 13, no. 1 (2009): 21–49.

15. Bullock and Culbert, "Coverage of Domestic Violence Fatalities."

16. A. Weiss and S. M. Chermak, "News Value of African-American Victims: An Examination of the Media's Presentation of Homicide," *Journal of Crime* 21, no. 2 (1998): 71–88.

17. Gina Damron and Joe Swickard, "Man Says He Was Paid to Kill Jane Bashara," *Detroit Free Press*, February 2, 2012.

18. Ibid.

19. The *Dateline NBC* program aired in May 2012 and was titled "Secrets in the Suburbs." Journalist Dennis Murphy provided details about the Jane Bashara homicide and interviewed both her husband and close family friends.

20. Michael Rosenfield, "Fight Breaks Out After the Arraignment; Tripod Broken and Used as a Weapon," *Channel 7 Action News WXYZ.com*.

21. Cecil Angel, "Mourners: 12-Year-Old Detroit Girl Killed Over a Phone Dreamed of a Bright Future," *Detroit Free Press*, February 11, 2012.

22. Tammy Stables Battaglia, "Mothers Seek Justice in Their Children's Slaying, Plead for Information," *Detroit Free Press*, February 22, 2012.

23. Angel, "Mourners."

24. C. A. Taylor and S. B. Sorenson, "The Nature of Newspaper Coverage of Homicide," *Injury Prevention* 8, no. 2 (2002): 121–27.

25. David Pritchard and Karen Hughes, "Patterns of Deviance in Crime News," *Journal of Communication* 47, no. 3 (1997): 49–67.

26. Sarah Escholz, Matthew Mallard, and Stacey Flynn, "Images of Prime Time Justice: A Content Analysis of *NYPD Blue* and *Law and Order*," *Journal of Criminal Justice and Popular Culture* 10, no. 3 (2004): 161–80; M. B. Oliver, "Caucasian Viewers' Memory of Black and White Criminal Suspects in the News," *Journal of Communications* 49, no. 3 (1999): 46–60.

27. Pritchard and Hughes, "Patterns of Deviance in Crime News."

28. Ibid.

CHAPTER 2. THE DESERVING VS. UNDESERVING VICTIM: CASE STUDIES OF BIASED MEDIA REPORTING AND LAW ENFORCEMENT INTERVENTION

1. Isabel Correia, Jorge Vala, and Patricia Aguiar, "The Effects of Belief in a Just World and Victim's Innocence on Secondary Victimization, Judgements of Justice and Deservingness," *Social Justice Research* 14, no. 3 (2001): 327–42.

2. Diane Richardson and Hazel May, "Deserving Victims? Sexual Status and the Social Construction of Violence," *Sociological Review* 47, no. 2 (1999): 308–31.

3. Melvin J. Lerner, *Belief in a Just World: A Fundamental Delusion* (New York: Plenum, 1980).

4. Correia, Vala, and Aguiar, "Effects of Belief in Just World."

5. Peter B. Kraska and Victor Kappeler, "To Serve and Pursue: Exploring Police Sexual Violence against Women," *Justice Quarterly* 12, no. 1 (1995): 86–111.

6. Vincent Price, David Tewksbury, and Elizabeth Powers, "Switching Trains of Thought: The Impact of News Frames on Readers' Cognitive Responses," *Communication Research* 24 (1997): 481–506; Phyllis A. Anastasio and Diana M. Costa, "Twice Hurt: How Newspaper Coverage May Reduce Empathy and Engender Blame for Female Victims of Crime," *Sex Roles* 51 (2004): 9–10.

7. Gary Moran and Brian L. Cutler, "The Prejudicial Impact of Pretrial Publicity," *Journal of Applied Social Psychology* 21, no. 5 (1991): 345–67.

8. F. James Davis, "Crime News in Colorado Newspapers," *American Journal of Sociology* 57, no. 4 (1952): 325–30, 326.

9. Sean Gardiner, "NYPD Inaction Over a Missing Black Woman Found Dead Sparks a Historic Racial-Bias Lawsuit," *Village Voice*, May 6, 2008. Gardiner's impressively thorough investigative report provides a significant amount of information on the kidnapping, torture, and rape of Romona Moore. There were no initial media reports about Moore's disappearance, and the first article written about the case was when her body was found, two weeks after she went missing.

10. Romona Moore's murder garnered a total ten articles in the *New York Times*— each article written after her decomposing body was found two weeks after her disappearance. None of the articles was written about her disappearance, as police did not notify the media until Moore's corpse was found under an abandoned ice cream truck only blocks from her home. Two of the articles appeared as metro brief articles on the case, with one of the short articles written to correct the spelling of her name.

11. Gardiner, "NYPD Inaction."

12. Ibid.

13. Rupe Simms, "Controlling Images and the Gender Construction of Enslaved African Women," *Gender and Society* 15, no. 6 (2001): 879–97.

14. Ibid.

15. Melissa V. Harris-Perry, *Sister Citizen: Shame, Stereotypes, and Black Women in America* (New Haven, Conn.: Yale University Press, 2011).

16. Toni Irving, "Decoding Black Women: Policing Practices and Rape Prosecution on the Streets of Philadelphia," *NWSA Journal* 20, no. 2 (2008): 101–19.

17. Jim Nolan, "Jury Rules against Schiebers in Lawsuit," *Philadelphia Daily News*, February 26, 2004.

18. Jasmine Owens, "'Historic' in a Bad Way: How the Tribal Law and Order Act Continues the American Tradition of Providing Inadequate Protection to American Indian and Alaska Native Rape Victims," *Journal of Criminal Law & Criminology* 102, no. 2 (2012): 497–524; Josephine Ross, "Blaming the Victim: 'Consent' within the Fourth Amendment and Rape Law," Harvard *Journal on Racial & Ethnic Justice* 26 (2010); Barbara L. Barnett, "How Newspapers Frame Rape Allegations: The Duke University Case," *Women & Language* 35, no. 2 (2012): 11–33; Linda Meyer Williams, "Race and Rape: The Black Woman as Legitimate Victim" (1986), ERIC, http://files.eric.ed.gov/fulltext/ED294970.pdf.

19. Harris-Perry, *Sister Citizen*; Irving, "Decoding Black Women."

20. "Witness Comes Back to Describe a Beating," *New York Times*, March 6, 2006.

21. Ibid.

22. Gardiner, "NYPD Inaction."

23. Ibid.

24. Ibid.

25. "New Yorker Is Missing after Walking Father's Dog," *New York Times*, March 5, 2003.

26. Ibid.

27. "Days after Woman Vanished, Clues Remain Scarce," *New York Times*, March 6, 2003.

28. "Gone in a Flash. Svetlana Aronov Disappeared from a Busy Street in Broad Daylight. Police Now Suspect Russian Mobsters," *People* 59, no. 15 (April 21, 2003): 77.

29. "Police Think Body in River May Be Woman Who Vanished," *New York Times*, May 7, 2003.

30. "Police Defend Differences in Searches for 2 Women," *New York Times*, May 14, 2003.

31. Ibid.

32. Ibid.

33. Gardiner, "NYPD Inaction."

34. John Marzulli, "Exclusive: Judge Nixes Claim of Racial Bias in Search of Missing Woman Found Dead in 2003," *New York Daily News*, August 4, 2014.

35. "Frustrations Grow as Probe into Greenville Teen's Murder Continues," WFAA.com–Dallas/Fort Worth/WFAA TV, November 9, 2012.

36. The Amber Alert (America's Missing: Broadcast Emergency Response System) was initiated in 1996 as an early warning system to incite community efforts to locate missing, abducted, and endangered children. It was named for Amber Hagerman, a nine-year-old white girl who was kidnapped and murdered while riding her bicycle. The program began in 1996 in Arlington, Texas, and by 2005 all fifty states adopted the Amber Alert program to protect missing children.

37. "Greenville Teen's Family Questions Police Response," WFAA.com—Dallas/Fort Worth/WFAA TV, November 6, 2012.

38. "Alicia Moore Sexually Assaulted Months before Homicide, Police Say," *Huffington Post*, November 9, 2012.

39. "Missing Person Report Reveals Why Greenville Police Didn't Issue Amber Alert," WFAA.com—Dallas/Fort Worth/WFAA TV, November 9, 2012.

40. Irving, "Decoding Black Women."

41. "Amber Alert Issued for Harris County Teen," *Houston Chronicle*, January 22, 2013.

42. "Haylie White, Missing 14-Year-Old Texas Girl, Believed to Be with 33-year Old Male Neighbor, Report Says," www.cbsnews.com.

43. "Man 33, Charged with Sexual Assault after He Runs Off with 14-Year-Old Girl Whose Family Had Taken Him In," *Daily Mail Newspaper Online*, January 23, 2013.

44. "Still Missing, but Amber Alert Cancelled: Haylie White, 14, Houston, TX," www.abc13.com.

45. "Hundreds March in Support of Slain Greenville Teen," WFAA.com—Dallas/Fort Worth/WFAA TV, November 10, 2012.

46. "The Final Moments of Tara's Life," *Detroit Free Press*, March 6, 2007.

47. "Could Skull Found in Brownstown be a Clue in Woman's 2007 Disappearance?" *Detroit Free Press*, February 22, 2013.

48. "Brownstown: Woman Missing Now for Two Years," *Herald News*, January 6, 2009.

49. In the *Detroit Free Press* alone, Tara Lynn Grant's story yielded seventy-three articles between February 18 and April 4, 2007. In contrast, there were only

seventeen articles in the same paper during the same time frame in the Lizzie Mae Collier-Sweet case.

50. "The Mr. Murderous Mom," *People* 67, no. 11 (March 19, 2007): 620.

51. Zlati Meyer, "In Search for Lizzie Mae, Police Hit a Road Block of Indifference," *Detroit Free Press*, March 12, 2007.

52. "Brownstown Twp.: Year Passes, Family Waits," *Detroit Free Press*, January 8, 2008.

53. Anahad O'Connor, "Body Identified as Missing Brooklyn Girl, 16," *New York Times*, June 24, 2006.

54. Joel Cairo, "4 Years Later, a Killer Is Still at Large: Chanel Petro-Nixon Is Dead, and It's Personal," *Daily News Opinion Page*, June 16, 2010.

55. Kareem Fahim, "In Bouncer's Murder Trial, Victim's Friend Recalls Their Last Night," *New York Times*, May 12, 2009.

56. James Barron, "Killing Reminded Bar's Manager of 'Preppie Murder' at His Family's Bar," *New York Times*, May 13, 2009.

57. Ibid.

58. Stephanie Gaskell, "Immette Law Is Passed—Licensing Bouncers," *New York Post*, August 17, 2006.

59. Laura Italiano and Dan Mangan, "Family of Murdered Student Imette St. Guillen Drops Fed Case for $130G," *New York Post*, March 26, 2011.

60. Gardiner, "NYPD Inaction."

61. E. Louis, "Follow Every Lead—'Runaways' May Be Murder Victims: Cops & Neighbors Must Step It Up," *New York Daily News*, June 24, 2007.

62. Rebecca Lopez and Steve Stoler, "Reward Offered as Investigation into Greenville Girl's Murder Continues," www.wfaa.com.

CHAPTER 3. AN UNEASY ALLIANCE: THE SYMBIOTIC RELATIONSHIP BETWEEN THE MEDIA AND LAW ENFORCEMENT

1. Robin Barton, "Missing White Women's Syndrome," *The Crime Report: Your Complete Criminal Justice Resource*, Investigative News Network, August 22,

2011. The *Crime Report* website is described as the only "comprehensive news service" dedicated to investigative journalism. The news source publishes articles, blogs, commentary, and criminal justice analysis on a regular basis and is managed by the Center on Media, Crime and Justice at John Jay College of Criminal Justice in New York City.

2. Ibid.

3. Ibid.

4. Lateef Mungin, "Cold Trail: Mother Still Seeking Answers in Daughter's Death," *Atlanta Journal-Constitution*, September 28, 2006.

5. Ibid.

6. Kathy Jefcoats, "No Suspects in Death of Troubled Teen Girl; Burned Body of 17-Year-Old Found Sept. 5," *Atlanta Journal-Constitution*, October 28, 2007.

7. David Pritchard and Karen Hughes, "Patterns of Deviance in Crime News," *Journal of Communication* 47, no. 3 (1997): 49–67; Moira Peelo, Brian Francis, Keith Soothill, Jayn Pearson, and Elizabeth Ackerley, "Newspaper Reporting and the Public Construction of Homicide," *British Journal of Criminology* 44 (2004): 256–75.

8. Pritchard and Hughes, "Patterns of Deviance."

9. Ibid.

10. Diane Richardson and Hazel May, "Deserving Victims? Sexual Status and the Social Construction of Violence," *Sociological Review* 47, no. 2 (1999): 308–31.

11. Richard J. Lundman, Olivia M. Douglass, and Jason Hanson, "News about Murder in the African-American Newspapers: Effects of Relative Frequency and Race and Gender Typifications," *Sociological Quarterly* 45, no. 2 (2004): 249–72.

12. Ibid.

13. Franklin D. Gilliam et al., "Crime in Black and White: The Violent, Scary World of Local News," *Harvard International Journal of Press/Politics* 1, no. 3 (1996): 6–23.

14. Ibid.

15. Richard J. Lundman, "The Newsworthiness and Selection Bias in News about Murder: Comparative and Relative Effects of Novelty and Race and Gender

Typifications on Newspaper Coverage of Homicide," *Sociological Forum* 18, no. 3 (2003): 357–86.

16. Timothy B. Lee, "The Unprofitability of the News Business Is a Sign of Success, Not Failure," *Washington Post*, September 26, 2013.

17. Lundman, "Newsworthiness and Selection Bias."

18. Ibid.

19. Ibid.

20. Linda Greenhouse, "Police Seek Clue to Stamford Murders," *The New York Times*, August 39, 1971. ProQuest Historical Newspapers: *The New York Times* (1851–2009)

21. Ibid.

22. Isabel Correia, Jorge Vala, and Patricia Aguiar, "The Effects of Belief in a Just World and Victim's Innocence on Secondary Victimization, Judgements of Justice and Deservingness," *Social Justice Research* 14, no. 3 (2001): 327–42.

23. Andrew Kidd and John Turk, "Suspect Arraigned in Strangulation Death of Pontiac Woman," *Oakland Press*, June 21, 2013.

24. Ibid.

25. Ibid.

26. "Star Jones Explains Rhonda Rules," Star Jones interview with *Huffington Post Live*, June 6, 2013.

27. Http://blog.napw.com/rhondas-rules-a-womans-guide-to-getting-her-affairs-in-order/.

CHAPTER 4. LOOKING AT MEDIA BIAS IN THREE MAJOR CITY NEWSPAPERS: RESULTS OF AUTHOR'S RESEARCH

1. An article in the *Washington Post* on October 26, 2009, reported that newspaper readership has reached a record decline—the lowest circulation record in seven decades. Frank Ahens, "The Accelerating Decline of Newspapers," *Washington Post*, October 26, 2009.

2. Quantitative data are data that are numerical, such as age, income, number of crimes, number of pages in an article, and so forth. Qualitative data are data

such as description of the murder of the victim as "brutal," marital status of the victim being mentioned, descriptions of the victim's personality ("she was well-liked"), the victim being described as a student, location of the article, and so forth. In short, quantitative data are data that can be readily described with numbers, while qualitative data describe qualities and context, data not easily described using numbers.

3. D. Riffe, S. Lacy, and F. G. Fico, *Analyzing Media Messages: Using Quantitative Content Analysis in Research* (London: Taylor & Francis, 2005); Klaus Krippendorf, "Reliability in Content Analysis: Some Common Misconceptions and Recommendations," *Human Communication Research* 30, no. 3 (2004): 411–33.

4. The first phase consisted of coding the articles for word count and location of the story in the newspaper (front page, front section, front of other section, and so forth) to generate data to test the mean (or average) between the two groups. These data would also be used to conduct a logistic regression analysis (a statistical method for prediction) to forecast race by word count, story location, number of photos, and marital status. Second, I attempted to assess the manner in which homicides of black and white victims were reported by enumerating (or counting) the number of story framing characteristics found in the articles across race.

5. David L. Altheide, "The News Media, the Problem Frame, and the Production of Fear," *Sociological Quarterly* 38, no. 4 (1997): 647–68.

6. The coding scheme of story framing characteristics I developed for the newspaper articles included the following: identification of where the article was found: *Front Page* (this section of the newspaper typically features stories that are considered important events that spark the reader's attention and generate an interest to read and purchase the rest of the newspaper); *Feature/Full Article* (a feature article is one that reports about an issue, person, or event with added depth and more background details); *Brief News Article* (I categorized a brief news article as one that contains less than 200 words); *Other/ Metro Section* (this section typically contains the citywide and countywide local news stories). Additionally, I noted whether the victim's death included excessive brutality (most newspaper articles contain descriptions of the manner in which the person was killed when these details are made available by

the coroner's office and police officials). A homicide that describes an injury to the victim that goes beyond what is necessary to end the person's life will be coded as excessive brutality. More specifically, I have identified the following indicators as excessive brutality: the victim was dismembered; the victim's body was burned or set on fire; or the victim suffered severe trauma as indicated by more than one method being used to cause harm (for example, stabbed and beaten, strangled and beaten, and so forth). Other story framing characteristics included: *Race of the Victim: Coded as "White," "Black," "Latina," or "Unable to Determine."* In assessing or determining the victim's race, in some cases a photo of the victim (if included in the article) was used. In other cases, race was inferred based on other characteristics in the story (that is, photos of family members of the victim or the surname or last name of the victim, such as "Munoz," which is associated with Hispanics). Additionally, a phone call was made to the reporter of the story to ascertain the victim's race, and this information was provided without consequence. When all reasonable avenues were exhausted and the victim's race could not be determined with any certainty, the victim's race was coded as "unable to determine." It should be noted that attempting to identify a victim's race by photos and surnames is not completely reliable, but doing so served as a reasonable surrogate in the absence of speaking with the victim's friends and family directly. *Age of the Victim*—the actual age of the victim in the article was coded as "under 30" (14–29), "30 and over," or "unable to determine." *Marital Status*—coded as "single," "married," "separated," "divorced," or "unable to determine." The following framing characteristics were binary coded with the number 1 for "yes" and 2 for "no": *Whether the article mentioned the victim's job or occupation* (2). *Whether the reporter interviewed friends, family, neighbors, or acquaintances of the victim. Whether there were references to personal characteristics that describe how others felt about the victim* (that is, popular, well-liked, smart, nice, and so forth). *Whether the article referred to the victim by first name. Whether the article indicated the victim's education level* (that is, college attended, degree, and so forth). *Whether high-ranking police/city officials* (chiefs, lieutenants, sergeants, county sheriffs, mayors, county prosecutors, and so forth) *commented on the case* (2). *Whether descriptive (emotionally charged adjectives) were used to describe the crime* (that is, "sad," "tragic," "brutal," "shocking," "unfortunate," and so forth). *Whether the story was featured on the front page of the edition. Whether the story was featured in the front section of the paper. Whether the story was featured in "front of other" section. Whether the story was featured in the "other" (or local) section of the paper. The number of words contained within the story (word count)*—coded as numeric scale variable—actual word count was entered in data spreadsheet. Pritchard and Hughes argued in their content analysis of newspapers that the article length and number of items published on a particular victim indicate whether a story is newsworthy (David Pritchard and Karen Hughes, "Patterns of Deviance in Crime News," *Journal of Communication* 47, no. 3 (1997): 49–67). *Whether a photo of the victim was included in the article*—coded as "yes" (1) or "no" (2). *Whether the article featured other photos* (that is, photos of family members, the accused perpetrator of the homicide, and so forth)— coded as "yes" (1) or "no" (2).

7. F. James Davis, "Crime News in Colorado Newspapers," *American Journal of Sociology* 57, no. 4 (1952): 325–30, 326.

8. Khalil Gibran Muhammad, *The Condemnation of Blackness: Race, Crime, and the Making of Modern Urban America* (Cambridge, Mass.: Harvard University Press, 2010). Muhammad profoundly argues that white foreign-born criminals were removed from UCR reports by the 1940s; as a result, blacks as deviants stood in stark contrast to whites, who represented "normalcy" when the two groups became the only categories of race tracked in FBI crime reports.

9. Laura Steinberg, "Metro Detroit Newspapers." About.com. http://detroit.about.com/od/media/tp/Detroit-Newspapers.htm.

The *Free Press* was ranked number 20 by Burelles Luce (a media relations and monitoring firm) in its top 100 daily newspapers for 2007 and had approximately 330,000 daily subscribers in contrast to the *Detroit News*, which ranked number 47 and had 202,000 daily subscribers. The *Free Press* has also been touted as being more liberal in its views and in the types of stories it covers compared to the more conservative *Detroit News*. One could reasonably assume that the *Detroit Free Press*, then, would have less racial bias in its framing of news stories and would thereby be a better source to collect the data for this study.

Correspondingly, the *Washington Post* and the *Atlanta Journal-Constitution* also ranked high on Burelles Luce's 2007 list—number 7 and 16, respectively. In 2007, the *Washington Post* had a daily circulation of close to 700,000 and the *Atlanta Journal-Constitution* had a daily circulation of 357,000. Both the *Washington Post* and the *Atlanta Journal-Constitution* are among the leading newspapers and are more widely distributed than other newspapers in their respective cities, such as the *Washington Times* (ranked 97) and the *Atlanta Business Chronicle*, which focuses primarily on local business news (and did not rank among the 100 top daily newspapers on the list).

10. However, none of the stories on white victims were featured on the front page, but they did appear within the front section of the newspaper. Articles on black victims were located in the "other" section more than 80 percent of the time.

11. Karin Brulliard, "Sterling Woman's Slaying Leaves Family Perplexed," *Washington Post*, January 25, 2005.

12. Cameron McWhirter, "Debutante's Slaying Splits Savannah—Downtown Crime: Response to Tragedy May Bring Change, but Highlights Racial, Economic Divide," *Atlanta Journal-Constitution*, January 8, 2006.

13. Kevin Michael Kruse, *White Flight: Atlanta and the Making of Modern Conservatism* (Princeton, N.J.: Princeton University Press, 2005).

14. Robert M. Bohm, "Capital Punishment in Two Judicial Circuits in Georgia," *Law and Human Behavior* 18, no. 3 (1994): 319–38; Giselle Corbie-Smith, Stephen B. Thomas, Mark V. Williams, and Sandra Moody-Ayers, "Attitudes and Beliefs of African-Americans toward Participation in Medical Research," *Journal of General Internal Medicine* 14, no. 9 (1999): 537–46; Ivy Kennelly, Joya Misra, and Marina Karides, "The Historical Context of Gender, Race, & Class in the Academic Labor Market," *Race, Gender & Class* (1999): 125–55; Robert D. Bullard, Glenn S. Johnson, and Angel O. Torres, eds., "Dismantling Transit Racism in Metro Atlanta," *Highway Robbery: Transportation Racism and New Routes to Equity*, 49–73 (Boston: South End Press, 2004).

15. Robert Edward Cochran, "Race, Place, and Identity: Examining Place Identity in the Racialized Landscape of Buckhead, Atlanta," *Geosciences Theses*, Paper 16 (2009).

CHAPTER 5. MAKING THE INVISIBLE VISIBLE: MINORITIES' EFFORTS TO OBTAIN RECOGNITION FOR FORGOTTEN VICTIMS

1. Richard Kahn and Douglas Kellner, "New Media and Internet Activism: From the 'Battle of Seattle' to Blogging," *New Media & Society* 6, no. 1 (2004): 87-95.

2. David Jacobs, "Internet Activism and the Democratic Emergency in the US," *Ephemera: Theory & Politics in Organization* 5, no. 1 (2005): 68-77; Kevin A. Hill and John E. Hughes, *Cyberpolitics: Citizen Activism in the Age of the Internet* (Lanham, Md.: Rowman & Littlefield, 1999); Jennifer Earl et al., "Changing the World One Webpage at a Time: Conceptualizing and Explaining Internet Activism," *Mobilization: An International Quarterly* 15, no. 4 (2010): 425-46.

3. Http://httpjournalsaolcomjenjer6steph.blogspot.com/2007/08/crimes-against-black-women-four-cases.html.

4. Cheryl Devall, "Women March in Boston, Protest Roxbury Killings," *Harvard Crimson*, April 30, 1979. The *Harvard Crimson* is a college newspaper published by Harvard University. It and the *Bay State Banner* were the only two newspapers that covered the series of murders of the twelve black female victims and the angry protests that followed. Neither paper enjoyed wide readership, such as the *Boston Globe*; thus the murders remained largely unknown to the general Boston public.

5. Wini Breines, *The Trouble between Us: An Uneasy History of White and Black Women in the Feminist Movement* (Oxford: Oxford University Press, 2006), 158.

6. Janis Kelly and Tacie Dejanikus, "Roxbury: Women Organizing against Violence," *Off Our Backs*, September. 30, 1979.

7. Alexis De Veaux, *Warrior Poet: A Biography of Audre Lorde* (New York: W. W. Norton, 2004).

8. Christine Pelisek, "Grim Sleeper's Sole Survivor," *LA Weekly News*, March 11, 2009.

9. http://www.cnn.com/SPECIALS/2009/news/grim.sleeper/index.html. Comments transcribed from CNN radio interview with Margaret Prescod in 2009 regarding Grim Sleeper serial murders of ten women in Los Angeles.

10. "L.A. Police Use Social Media to Get ID Help on Possible 'Grim Sleeper' Victims," *CNN Justice News*, October 12, 2012.

11. Pelisek, "Grim Sleeper's Sole Survivor."

12. Christine Pelisek, "The Grim Sleeper's Trial Is Moving at Snail's Pace, and Victims' Families Are Furious," *Daily Beast*, March 21, 2013.

13. "Man Charged with Slayings in N.C. Sought in Kitsap Case—Investigators Blame Him for 10 Murders Over 20 Months," *Seattle Times*, March 14, 1994.

14. Http://www.trutv.com/library/crime/serial_killers/predators/wallace. True crime library provided a synopsis of the Henry Louis Wallace Jr. serial murder case, detailing specifics about the victims and rape/murders that occurred in from 1992 to 1994 in the Charlotte-Mecklenburg area of North Carolina. In my attempts to access archival data from the *Charlotte-Observer* about the murders, I found it difficult to locate a single article about the murders.

15. Peter Applebome, "2 Years, 10 Murders and 1 Question," Special to the *New York Times*. *New York Times (1923–Current file)*.

16. Ibid.

17. Corky Siemaszko, "Brooklyn Marine Sergeant & Wife Tortured, Slain in Calif.; 4 of His Men Arrested," *New York Daily News*, November 6, 2006.

18. Nancy Dillon and Corky Siemaszko, "'Nobody Deserves Death Like This,' Says DA in Torture, Slaying of Marine, Wife," *New York Daily News*, November 8, 2006.

19. Nancy Dillon and Corky Siemaszko, "Cold-Blooded Details of Brooklyn Marine and Wife's Brutal Murder Revealed in California Courtroom," *New York Daily News*, June 18, 2009.

20. Gina McCauley, "Why? Quiana Jenkins-Pietrzak Week—Day #1 Identifying Morally Indifferent Reporters," *What About Our Daughters?.com*, June 10, 2013.

21. Gina McCauley, "Quiana Jenkins-Pietrzak Week Day 3: Reuters Responds—Share Your Responses," *What About Our Daughters?.com*, June 14, 2013.

22. *The Cheshire Murders*, HBO film, 2013.

23. Gina McCauley, email interview by author, August 27, 2013.

CONCLUSION

1. Hilary Moss, "Satoshi Kanazawa Causes Firestorm after Claiming Black Women Less Attractive," *Huffington Post*, May 17, 2011.

2. Dennis T. Lowry, Tarn Ching Josephine Nio, and Dennis W. Leitner, "Setting the Public Fear Agenda: A Longitudinal Analysis of Network TV Crime Reporting, Public Perceptions of Crime, and FBI Crime Statistics," *Journal of Communication* 53, no. 1 (2006): 67–73; Mark Warr, "Fear of Crime in the United States: Avenues for Research and Policy," *Criminal Justice* (0887–7785) 4 (2000): 451–90; Allen E. Liska, "Fear of Crime and Constrained Behavior Specifying and Estimating a Reciprocal Effects Model," *Social Forces* (0037–07732) 66 (1987): 827–37.

3. Gordon Trowbridge and Oralander Brand-Williams, "The Costs of Racial Segregation Part I: Racial Attitudes," *Detroit Free Press*, January 14, 2002.

4. Thomas Hargrove, "Victims Age, Sex, Race Affect Homicide Clearance Rates," *Scripps Howard News Service*.

INDEX